MW00606177

# IS THERE LIFE IN OUTER SPACE?

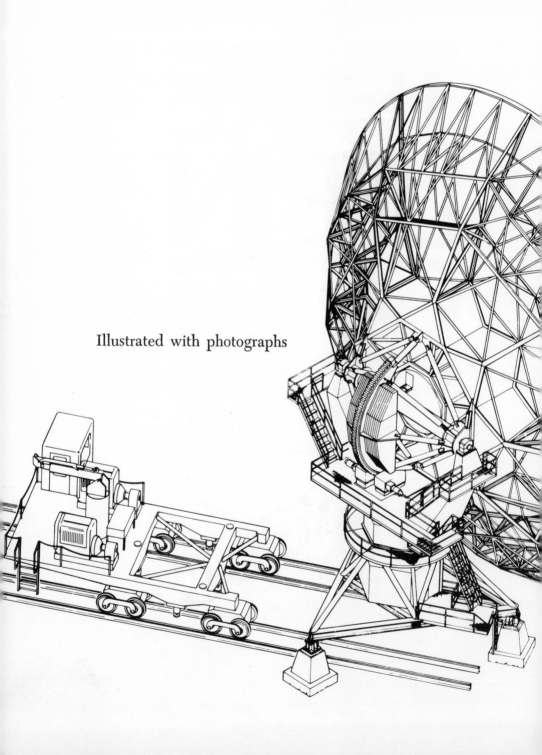

Illustrated with photographs

# IS THERE LIFE IN OUTER SPACE

## BY
## ROBERT KRASKE

Harcourt Brace Jovanovich
New York and London

## by the same author

*The Story of the Dictionary*
(published by Harcourt Brace Jovanovich)

*Crystals of Life: The Story of Salt*
(published by Doubleday & Company)

*Silent Sentinels: The Story of Locks, Vaults and Burglar Alarms*
(published by Doubleday & Company)

*The Treason of Benedict Arnold, September 1780*
(published by Franklin Watts)

*The Statue of Liberty Comes to America*
(published by Garrard Publishing Company)

*America the Beautiful: Stories of Patriotic Songs*
(published by Garrard Publishing Company)

*Harry Houdini: Master of Magic*
(published by Garrard Publishing Company)

Title page illustration courtesy of *National Science Foundation*

Printed in the United States of America

First edition

B C D E F G H I J K

Library of Congress Cataloging in Publication Data

Kraske, Robert
Is there life in outer space?

Bibliography: p.
SUMMARY: Examines evidences of and theories about
life on other planets.
1. Life on other planets—Juvenile literature.
[1. Life on other planets]  I. Title.
QB54.K7        574.99'9        76-929
ISBN 0-15-239190-8

# Contents

For Bill and Eleanor Knox

# Acknowledgments

Many people contributed material that was used in the preparation of this book. In particular I would like to thank:

Beacon Press for permission to reprint statements, on pages 21-23, 26, 32, 65, and 72, by Dr. Harlow Shapley from his book *Of Stars and Men* (Rev. ed., 1964).

Professor Richard Berendzen, Department of Astronomy, Boston University, for his statement on page 3.

Dr. Melvin Calvin, Director, Laboratory of Chemical Biodynamics, University of California, Berkeley, for his statement on page 67.

Mr. Norman Cousins, Editor, *Saturday Review*. His statement on page 66 appeared in the November 30, 1974, issue of *Saturday Review;* his statement on page 71 appeared in the January 11, 1975, issue of *Saturday Review*. Both are used with Mr. Cousins's permission.

Doubleday & Company, Inc., for permission to reprint statements on pages 21, 26, 34, and 74 by Dr. Carl Sagan from his book *The Cosmic Connection: An Extraterrestrial Perspective* (1973).

Dr. Frank Drake, Director, National Astronomy and Ionosphere Center, Cornell University, for his statements on pages 64 and 70-71.

Mr. Kendrick Frazier, Editor, *Science News,* for his statement on page 71.

Professor Charles H. Hapgood, Winchester, New Hampshire, for his recollection of an afternoon's discussion with Albert Einstein, pages 4-5.

Dr. J. Allen Hynek, Professor of Astronomy, Northwestern University, and Director, Center for UFO Studies, Evanston, Illinois, for his statement on page 14.

Dr. Robert Jastrow, Director, Goddard Institute for Space Studies, New York City, for his statement on page 4 from "Are We Alone in the Cosmos?" by Robert Jastrow, *Natural History*, June–July 1974.

Macmillan Publishing Co., Inc., for permission to reprint two statements from books by John W. Macvey. The first, page 15, is from *Whispers in Space*, Copyright © 1973 by John W. Macvey. The second, pages 25-26, is from *Alone in the Universe?*, © John W. Macvey 1963.

McGraw-Hill Book Company, Inc., for permission to quote two statements, pages 67 and 73, by Walter Sullivan from his book *We Are Not Alone: The Search for Intelligent Life on Other Worlds* (1965).

Random House, Inc., for permission to reprint two statements, pages 18 and 69, by John G. Taylor from his book *Black Holes: The End of the Universe?*, Copyright © 1973 by John Taylor.

*Redbook Magazine* for permission to reprint two statements by Dr. Margaret Mead on pages 13 and 15, from "UFOs —Visitors from Outer Space?" by Margaret Mead (reprinted from *Redbook Magazine*, September 1974. Copyright © 1974 by The Redbook Publishing Company).

Professor George Wald, Biological Laboratories, Harvard University, for his statements on pages 30-31 and 31-32.

Special thanks also go to the following people who provided photographs and special material for this book:

Ms. Connie Bart, Office of Public Information, Cornell University.

David L. Moore, Director, Public Information Office, Kitt Peak National Observatory, Tucson, Arizona.

Wallace R. Oref, Public Education Officer, National Radio Astronomy Observatory, Green Bank, West Virginia.

# IS THERE LIFE IN OUTER SPACE?

# 1

# "A Matter for Investigation"

"The Galaxy, that Milky Way . . .
Powdered with Stars."
—John Milton, *Paradise Lost*

Have you ever gazed at a night sky sprinkled with stars and wondered, "Is there life out there? Are there people on other planets looking at the very same stars? Are we on Earth the only intelligent beings in the universe? Is there life in outer space?"

If you have ever pondered thoughts like these, you would join a long line of curious people stretching back through centuries who have asked the same questions.

In the fourth century B.C., a Greek wise man named Metrodorus wrote: "To consider the earth as the only populated world in infinite space is as absurd as to assert that, in an entire field sown with millet, only one grain will grow!"

On a starry night two hundred years before Columbus discovered America, a Chinese scholar, Teng Mu, stood in a walled courtyard and said to himself: "How unreasonable it would be to suppose that, besides the earth and the sky which we can see, there are no other skies and no other earths!"

In China the question was safe to ask, but not in Europe. The bishops in the Church didn't like it when Giordano Bruno, a mere priest, boldly stated: "Innumerable suns exist! Innumerable earths circle around their suns, no worse and no less inhabited than this globe of ours. For no reasonable mind can assume that heavenly bodies which may be far more magnificent than ours would not bear upon them creatures similar or even superior to those upon our human Earth."

The bishops warned Bruno: "You are speaking against the teachings of the Church! The Earth as everyone knows is the center of the universe! Other earths? Other creatures more intelligent? A grave sin to preach such error!"

In February 1600, the bishops ordered Bruno tied to a stake and sticks and brush piled to his knees. But before the torch was applied, the brave priest had the final word: "I await your sentence with less fear than you pass it," he told his judges. "The time will come when all will see what I see!"

In the nineteenth century, the belief that intelligent beings inhabited other planets was so strong that two European astronomers hatched schemes to contact them.

In Austria, Joseph von Littrow proposed digging canals in the Sahara Desert in the shape of triangles 20 miles long on a side. "We'll flood them with water," he said, "then float a film of kerosene on top. At night, we touch a match to the kerosene. *Whoom!* All the triangles light up! On Mars they'll see our great figures and know that on Earth there live intelligent beings!"

In France, Charles Gros came up with another idea. He drew elaborate plans for a giant mirror. "A mirror of this size," he assured government officials, "will reflect sunlight all the way to Mars. *Voilà!* We transmit signals to the Martians!"

Von Littrow's canals were never dug and Gros's marvelous mirror was never built, but scientists and scholars alike continued to ask the same question: Is there life in outer space?

Today, in the second half of the twentieth century, scientists have begun to answer this question.

In November 1972, at a meeting at Boston University on

the subject of Life Beyond Earth, an astronomer, Professor Richard Berendzen, told the audience: "The question has become not so much one of *if* [life exists] as of *where*. And many of these forms of life are probably more technically advanced than our own selves."

And in the same year, the National Academy of Sciences published a report that in part said:

"Each passing year has seen our estimates of this probability of life in space increase, along with our capabilities for detecting it. More and more scientists feel that contact with other civilizations is no longer something beyond our dreams, but a natural event in the history of mankind that will perhaps occur within the lifetime of many of us. . . . At this instant, through this very document, are passing radio waves bearing the conversations of distant creatures, conversations that we could record if we but pointed a radio telescope in the right direction and tuned it to the proper frequency."

Other distinguished scientists have stated:

"Life is a cosmos-wide phenomenon!"

"I think there is no question that we live in an inhabited universe that has life all over it!"

"Rough calculations lead us to expect at least one million intelligent civilizations in our galaxy."

Scientists are normally cautious. They want to see evidence —positive proof—before they commit themselves. What makes scientists today so sure that life exists on planets other than Earth? Have they found proof?

No. No proof, no evidence. ("Absence of evidence," said one scientist, "is not evidence of absence.") But what they have found is circumstantial evidence—evidence that points to the inescapable conclusion that, yes, life does exist on other planets. There is simply no other conclusion to come to. But proof? That can come only when we actually make contact with other intelligent beings in the universe.

This interest in the possibility of life in outer space has created a new science—exobiology, the study of extraterrestrial life. Extraterrestrial means simply "beyond Earth." But exo-biology is unlike other sciences. Other sciences work with real things—like chemical formulas or steel beams or jet engines. "Exobiology," said one astronomer, "has yet to demonstrate that its subject matter exists!"

But what if life in outer space doesn't exist? Despite cir-cumstantial evidence and educated opinions by experienced scientists, the question must remain open until proof is actually found.

"Scientists tend to feel that . . . the existence of life here proves that life, and even intelligence, must be common to the universe," said Dr. Robert Jastrow, Director of the Goddard Institute for Space Studies. "While I share their optimism, there are no objective grounds for it; only the wishful thought that life will arise wherever conditions allow. The contrary might be true; the evolution of life . . . may be a near-miracle of extremely low probability; the earth may be the only planet so favored in this galaxy and, perhaps, in the cosmos."

In the year before his death in 1955, the famous scientist Albert Einstein was visited at his home in Princeton, New Jersey, by Professor Charles Hapgood of Keene State College in New Hampshire. The two professors spent an entire after-noon talking.

During the conversation, the question came up of how scientists should approach new ideas.

Dr. Einstein said that it was "always a mistake to reject a new theory out of hand no matter how improbable or even im-possible it might appear. There might be a germ of truth mixed with the dross."

Hapgood recalled that Einstein felt that by having preset opinions and by failing to examine new ideas carefully, a scien-tist—or any other questioning person, for that matter—could lose valuable clues to truth.

Then the two professors talked about the question of life on other planets. "It should not be dismissed," Einstein said thoughtfully. "It must be taken seriously as a matter for investigation."

And so our story investigates why astronomers, biologists, chemists, and other scientists believe intelligent beings exist "out there" in the vast reaches of the universe and what those beings might be like.

Another part of our story tells about the remarkable instruments scientists plan to use to communicate with other worlds in space. At this moment, as you read this sentence, messages from Earth are zinging into space at incredible speed. They are saying: "We are here. We are ready to talk to you. Answer, please!"

Our story also inquires into another question that has mystified people for ages: Are intelligent beings from other planets visiting Earth today? Has Earth been visited in the past by intelligent beings? Are Unidentified Flying Objects— "flying saucers"—real?

Finally, our story looks into the possible good that may come from communicating with intelligent beings elsewhere in the universe. Could they help us leapfrog hundreds, possibly thousands, of years in learning about the universe? Can they tell us if *other* universes exist beyond our universe or if it's possible to travel *faster* than light? Do they know what "black holes" are—the mysterious voids in space that draw all matter, including spacecraft, into them and from which nothing can ever escape?

"You must recognize that we don't know this field," said a physics professor at an eastern university who has studied the universe for years. "Many surprises, even the most extraordinary surprises, are possible!"

# 2

# UFOs: Real or Unreal?

---

"I consider a visit to our
planet by an extraterrestrial
race to be extremely probable."
—Hermann Oberth, pioneer
of modern rocketry

---

June 24, 1947. As Ken Arnold was flying his small plane near Mount Rainier, Washington, he suddenly peered in disbelief through the windshield. Could he really believe what his eyes told him? Ahead was something that in all his years as a pilot he had never seen before—nine gleaming disc-shaped objects, each about 100 feet wide, flying in formation past his line of flight. They were moving fast—about 1,200 m.p.h. he guessed.

Landing at Yakima, Arnold described his strange experience to workers at the field. Someone phoned newspapers and by the following day people across the United States read about "flying saucers," a term coined by a reporter who covered the story.

In the 30 years that have passed since Arnold's "sighting," over 60,000 UFOs have been sighted in the United States alone.

In 1948, the U.S. Air Force began looking into the phenomenon of UFOs. Twenty years later, Air Force investigators had checked into 11,108 UFO sightings. Ninety-four percent or 10,432 turned out to be "misidentifications"—helicopters, jet planes, weather balloons, orbiting space satellites, bright stars, comets, fireballs, meteors, flights of geese, sunlight glowing on ice crystals in cirrus clouds, and mirages caused by light waves bending as they passed through layers of cold and warm air.

A few sightings were outright hoaxes. Two high school boys tied lighted candles to weather balloons and launched them. Wind currents drifted the balloons, glowing orange, across the night sky. Suddenly each one disappeared in a puff of smoke. Result? People for miles around phoned sheriffs' offices to report UFOs.

Some sightings turned out to be visions of mentally disturbed persons. A Los Angeles woman claimed she had gone for a spin in a UFO with Venusians. She described them as being "unimaginably beautiful." Why hadn't anyone else seen these visitors to Earth? She drew herself up haughtily. They were visible only to "the pure of heart and spirit," she announced.

These misidentifications, hoaxes, and hallucinations tended to discredit UFOs. Who could possibly take them seriously after investigation of thousands of sightings turned up results like these?

In 1968, the director of the Air Force study, Dr. Edward U. Condon, a former physics professor at the University of Colorado, turned in his report. It said in part:

"Careful consideration of the record . . . leads us to conclude that further extensive study of UFOs probably cannot be justified in the expectation that science will be advanced thereby. . . . No direct evidence whatever of a convincing nature now exists for the claim that any UFOs represent spacecraft visiting earth from another civilization."

With the publication of Dr. Condon's report, the Air Force stopped investigating UFO sightings. But not all scientists agreed with the report. The American Institute of Aeronautics and Astronautics, an organization of scientists and engineers, stated that it "did not find a basis in the report . . . that nothing of scientific value will come of further study" of UFOs. The government should continue to collect and analyze data on UFOs, it urged.

And what about the 6 percent or 676 UFO sightings that hadn't been identified by Air Force investigators? Some certainly suggested that strange objects were flying around in our skies. For example:

• While on a train west of Reno, Nevada, a University of Minnesota astronomer saw—in full daylight—a UFO flying parallel with the train just above a ridge of nearby mountains. The craft was visible for four or five minutes, then rose out of sight and disappeared. "I'm familiar with such things as flights of wild geese, balloons, temperature inversions, and the sun shining through the clouds," he said. "I do not suffer from hallucinations. I saw a UFO."

• Over Washington National Airport, five radar operators tracked UFOs on three different radar sets. The crafts were moving at speeds from 100 to 800 m.p.h. Four airline pilots, approaching the field for a landing, saw the same luminous objects. This was an example of a sighting made by trained observers, each one independent of the others. None had anything particular to gain from reporting the sighting.

• Two police sergeants in Socorro, New Mexico, investigated a report of a UFO outside town. They saw "a metallic, egg-shaped object" 12 to 15 feet long standing on four short legs in a gulley. As they approached, bright blue flame spurted from the bottom of the craft, and it rose from the gulley into the sky and sped away. The astonished officers examined the sand and found four indentations each about three and a half inches deep where the metal legs had stood. Bushes around the gulley, they reported, were charred and smoking.

• Entire crowds have also sighted UFOs. At an air show at Longview, Washington, as people watched a sky-writing plane, a UFO appeared, followed by two more. The manager of the show, a former commander in the U.S. Navy, announced the sightings on the public address system. Pilots, engineers, and police officers watched the craft through binoculars. Many reported that they seemed to flutter and waver as they maneuvered over the field. Twenty minutes after the first ones appeared, two more flew up, then all five sped away.

• U.S. astronauts, during the pre-moon flight Gemini tests in 1965, saw UFOs on three occasions.

On the June 3–7 Gemini 4 flight, astronaut James McDivitt reported a long, cylindrical object "white or silver in appearance as seen against the day sky" over the Pacific Ocean with what appeared to be antennas extending from it.

On the next orbit, he radioed: "Just saw a satellite very high . . . just like a star on the ground when you see one go by, a long, long ways away."

Ground control reported no satellites in the area. The nearest satellite, Pegasus, was over 1,200 miles away. Empty fuel tanks from rockets launched before the Gemini flights? On that day, there were ten in space, but at distances from 263 to 587 miles away and unsightable. Besides, the UFO McDivitt had seen was traveling in a south-to-north direction. Satellites and other space debris would be orbiting Earth in an east-to-west direction.

In December, Frank Borman in Gemini 7 reported a "bogey at 10 o'clock high." ("Bogey" is Air Force slang for "unidentified aircraft.")

Ground control replied: "Please check to see if bogey is your booster rocket accompanying you in orbit."

Jim Lovell, in Gemini 7 with Borman, interrupted. "I have the booster on *my* side," he said. "It's a brilliant body in the sun, against the black background" of the sky. He could see it slowly tumbling as it orbited Earth with their spacecraft.

The UFO continued to fly in formation on Borman's side, then suddenly disappeared. The incident took place on the second orbit on the first day of the 14-day Gemini 7 flight.

What did Dr. Condon's report say about the astronauts' three UFO sightings?

9

"The training and perspicacity of the astronauts put their reports of sightings in the highest category of credibility. Trained to deal in facts only, they avoided personal interpretations of what they saw. The three unexplained sightings . . . are a challenge to the analyst."

## Sky Ships Long Ago

Most people believe UFOs are a recent event, that they first appeared in U.S. skies when Ken Arnold saw the nine "flying saucers" over Washington in mid-1947. But the truth is that people have been seeing strange objects in the sky for centuries. "Countless times in geological history," wrote Arthur C. Clarke, a famous science writer, "strange ships may have drifted down through the skies of earth."

Legends and ancient writings of many people—in India, Japan, and Tibet, for example—tell of beings who came to Earth thousands of years ago in metal craft.

In the first three chapters of the Book of Ezekiel in the Old Testament, the sixth-century prophet described a visit to Earth from what might have been extraterrestrial beings in a spaceship:

"And I looked, and, behold, a whirlwind came out of the north, a great cloud, and a fire unfolding itself, and a brightness was about it. . . .

"Also out of the midst thereof came the likeness of four living creatures. And this was their appearance; they had the likeness of a man. . . .

"And their feet were straight feet; and the sole of their feet was like the sole of a calf's foot: and they sparkled like the color of burnished brass."

Some three hundred years later, a Babylonian priest and historian named Berosus recorded the ancient legends of the Sumerians, who may have been the world's first civilized people, and suggested some answer to one of the grand unsolved mysteries of the ages: How did human beings become civilized?

Before the Sumerians, people "lived without rule and order, like beasts of the field," according to Berosus. To Sumer on the shores of the Persian Gulf came a strange being out of the sea called Oannes—"an animal endowed with reason." Oannes talked with the Sumerians and gave them "an insight into letters and sciences and every kind of art. He taught them to construct houses, to found temples, to compile laws, and explained to them the principles of geometrical knowledge. He made them distinguish the seeds of the earth, and showed them how to collect fruits. In short, he instructed them in everything which could tend to soften manners and humanize mankind."

Was Oannes a visitor from another planet? No one knows for sure. Sumerian legends state only that non-humans taught them mathematics, astronomy, agriculture, and law and helped them make the transition from a hunter-like society to—in about 3500 B.C.—what was probably the world's first civilization. The mystery is: How did it happen so suddenly? A professor at Harvard wrote: "Overnight, as it were, [Sumerian] civilization crystallized."

Were visitors from another world in space the ancestors of the Ainu (*eye-noo*) who live on Hokkaidō, the northernmost island of Japan?

"These mysterious people have long been a puzzle," an anthropologist said recently. "Where did they come from—and when?" (An anthropologist studies the origins and customs of people.)

Unlike the Japanese, the Ainu do not have Mongoloid ancestors. Their eyes are round, their skin fair, and the men have thick facial hair.

Some anthropologists believe that the Ainu may be a separate race entirely. Farmers and fishermen, the 300 remaining Ainu on Hokkaidō today may be the last survivors of a people who have lived on the island for at least 7,000 years.

Their own belief about their origin has passed verbally from parents to children for thousands of years because their special language has no written form. According to the anthropologist who studied them for years, they believe that "their ancestors were space people—the same who still live in the clouds and send those flying saucers to earth."

On a hill in the Saru River valley on Hokkaidō stands a monument to this legend. The inscription says: "This is the place where the first Ainu came to Earth."

In U.S. skies, strange craft have been seen for almost 350 years. In 1639 and again in 1644, the governor of Massachusetts John Winthrop reported UFOs over Boston harbor. The first, a glowing object about nine feet wide, maneuvered over the Charles River, darting, zooming, zigzagging, and hovering for two to three hours, he recorded in his journal.

The second sighting was of two UFOs. The first flew in from the northeast about eight o'clock in the evening, and the second came from the east. Over Noddle's Island in Boston harbor, the two maneuvered together. "One would close in on the other, then part and close in again diverse times," Winthrop recorded, "and so until finally they dipped behind the hill in the island and vanished."

April 1897 seemed to be a month for UFO sightings. People in Kansas, Missouri, Texas, Nebraska, and Colorado reported seeing strange objects in the sky. A newspaper, the *New York Herald,* stated that, betwen 8:00 P.M. and 2:00 A.M. on the night of April 9-10, "thousands of amazed persons [in Chicago] declared that the lights seen in the northwest were those of an airship, or some floating object, miles above the earth."

Late in World War II, bomber crews in Europe described "blobs of light" accompanying them on their missions. So often were these sightings made that airmen began calling them "foo fighters." Both Allied and German intelligence agents said the objects were secret weapons being tested by the *other* side. This explanation turned out to be untrue, but no other explanation was ever made. When the war ended, the "foo fighters" were forgotten.

Since World War II, UFOs have been sighted in most countries. Pilots of Japanese airliners reported being followed by UFOs far out over the Pacific. German pilots observed UFOs keeping pace with them as they flew over the North Sea. Near Staffordshire, England, 70 sightings were reported in one ten-week period. In 1954, thousands of people in Rome watched a cigar-shaped object maneuver over the city; at the airport, radar operators tracked the UFO on their scopes.

In 1967, Felix Ziegel of the Moscow Institute of Aviation stated at a conference on space civilizations: "We have well-documented sightings from every corner of the U.S.S.R. It's hard to believe that all are optical illusions. Illusions don't register clearly on photographic plates and radar."

And in the United States, astronaut Gordon Cooper said: "People have seen flying saucers at close hand, and in many cases they have been verified on radar. It is ridiculous to say that they're all completely unreal."

Anthropologist Margaret Mead said: "Yes, there are unidentified flying objects. These are phenomena that, even after the most cautious and painstaking investigations, cannot be explained away. This much, at least, we must accept."

But many people who believe UFOs exist have never seen one. "Why," they ask, "have farmers, pilots, police officers, and people just walking down the street seen one and I haven't?"

A scientist who has spent years investigating UFOs answered the question this way: "Every year there are 35,000 to 40,000 fatal car accidents in the U.S. That's somewhere between 670 and 770 people killed each week. And yet I have been driving on streets and highways for over 30 years and I have yet to see a car accident in which someone gets killed. But I know they happen—hundreds of times each week. The country is just too big. There's too many places for accidents to happen. I may never see one."

## The Most Reasonable Explanation
What, then, are UFOs? There are various explanations.
- Some UFOs have been identified as hoaxes and frauds.
- Misidentification of natural phenomena—meteors, satel-

lites, fireballs, mirages, etc.—account for some sightings.

• Mass hallucination or "seeing things" may explain some UFOs, but it simply does not provide the answer for cases in which there are visual and radar sightings and cases of simultaneous sightings over a large area by people unknown to each other.

• Secret weapons or secret aircraft might have served as an answer during the first few years of the sightings, but keeping a weapon or aircraft secret over 30 years is not possible. Word would leak out.

• Perhaps UFOs are something entirely unknown to us. This view has been expressed best by J. Allen Hynek, Professor of Astronomy at Northwestern University and Director of the Center for UFO Studies in Evanston, Illinois. Testifying before the House Committee on Science and Astronautics of the U.S. Congress in 1968, Dr. Hynek stated that "the UFO problem may not lend itself to an immediate solution in our time. The problem may be far more complex than we imagine. Attempts to solve the problem may be no more productive than attempts to solve the problem of the Aurora Borealis would have been 100 years ago. The cause of the northern lights could not have been determined in the framework of the science of 1868. Scientific knowledge in those days was not sufficient to encompass the phenomenon."

• UFOs may actually be observation craft from other civilizations in space. While scientists recognize that no evidence exists to support this view, there are those who believe it to be the most reasonable explanation for UFOs.

In a newspaper interview, rocket pioneer Dr. Hermann Oberth said: "These objects [UFOs] are conceived and directed by intelligent beings of a very high order. They probably do not originate in our solar system, perhaps not even in our galaxy."

Appearing before the same committee of Congress as Dr. Hynek, the late Dr. James McDonald, a physicist at the University of Arizona, said: "My position is that UFOs are entirely real and we do not know what they are. . . . The possibility that these are extraterrestrial devices, that we are dealing with surveillance from some advanced technology, is a possibility I take very seriously. . . . You have a feeling you are dealing with some very high technology, devices of an entirely real nature which defy explanation in terms of present-day science."

Another scientist, this one from the Westinghouse Astronuclear Laboratory, told the committee: "I have concluded that the earth is being visited by intelligently controlled vehicles whose origin is extraterrestrial. This doesn't mean I know where they come from, why they are here, or how they operate."

If, then, we take the last possibility—surveillance by extraterrestrial beings or spacecraft—as the most reasonable explanation for UFOs, other questions immediately come up.

"Why don't they get in touch with us?" people ask. "Why don't they land right on the White House lawn and declare themselves!"

In reply, scientists say that, while this may be what *we* want, it may not necessarily be what *they* want.

"The most likely explanation, it seems to me," said Dr. Mead, "is that they are simply watching what we are up to— that a responsible society outside our solar system is keeping an eye on us to see that we don't set in motion a chain reaction that might have repercussions far outside our solar system."

"Since the late 1940s," said John W. Macvey, a Fellow of the Royal Astronomical Society, "we have been in possession of dangerous nuclear toys. More recently a 'primitive' capability in space exploration has appeared. To a grand cosmic federation all this might seem faintly ominous. It might seem to constitute a situation worth watching."

A melding of opinions from other scientists might go like this:

"Why *should* they want to get in touch with us! We may feel we're more important in the universe and to 'them' than in truth we really are! They may want to observe us only and not interfere with the development of our civilization. They may not care if we see them; but they also may not care to say 'hello.'

"Thirty years of observation may seem a long time to us, but to them these years may be the same as only a few hours or minutes to us, especially if they measure their life spans in centuries. After all, fruit flies here on earth live only a few days; elephants live over a hundred years. It is possible that life spans of people on Earth and of intelligent creatures on other planets in space would show similar differences."

Some scientists have suggested that Earth is a kind of galactic zoo or wildlife preserve. Just as we set aside wilderness areas and wildlife sanctuaries to allow animals and growing things to develop naturally while we observe them, so perhaps Earth was set aside ages ago for the same purpose.

These scientists say: "The perfect zoo would be one in which the 'specimens' inside do not interact with, and are unaware of, their zookeepers. Nor does the zookeeper make himself known to his charges."

Are we being observed by intelligent beings from other civilizations in the universe? Are they watching our progress in space travel and our use of nuclear weapons? Do we live in a galactic "zoo" observed by our "keepers," but having no communication with them?

Never before in our history have we had to confront ideas like these. The simple fact is that we who have always regarded ourselves as supreme in the universe may not be so. Now we have to recognize that, among the stars in the heavens, there may very well be worlds inhabited by beings who are as superior to us as we are to ants.

# 3

# The Search for Life on Other Worlds in Space

> "But who shall dwell in these
> worlds if they be inhabited? . . .
> Are we or they Lords of the World?"
> —Johannes Kepler (1571–1630),
> German astronomer

Gazing at the planet Venus one night three centuries ago, the French writer de Fontenelle said to a companion, "I can tell from here . . . what the inhabitants of Venus are like; they resemble the moors of Granada; a small black people, burned by the sun, full of wit and fire, always in love, writing verse, fond of music, arranging festivals, dances, and tournaments every day."

A cartoon in a national magazine a few years ago presented another picture of extraterrestrial beings. A creature from another planet—bug eyes, green skin, floppy antennae—peers nearsightedly at the glass globe of a gumball machine and asks, "What's a nice girl like you doing in a place like this?"

Today, when scientists imagine what life on other worlds in space might be like, they avoid poetic inventions like de Fontenelle's or jokes about baldheaded creatures with green skin. Instead, they base their ideas on the findings of scientists in many different fields—astronomy, biology, chemistry, physics, and mathematics. Not one would try to draw a picture of extraterrestrial beings, but they can make some intelligent guesses about what they must look like. The only thing they are certain of is that they are "out there."

Said Cornell University astronomer Frank D. Drake: "The probability is 100 percent that there is life beyond the solar system."

Someone then asked Dr. Drake what he thought the probability was of *intelligent* life elsewhere in the universe.

"I think that's 100 percent also," he replied.

John Taylor, professor of mathematics at the University of London, wrote: "It is very likely that there are many life-supporting planets even in our own galaxy, with a proportion of them bearing intelligent beings. Such life may be very different from the varieties which have developed on our globe, and could have a very different view of the universe from our own."

What makes scientists like Professor Taylor and Dr. Drake so sure? Maybe they are making a mistake. Maybe we *are* alone in the universe. For centuries scientists and philosophers alike have argued that life was too complex to evolve anywhere except by a wild accident or a marvelous act of creation. Earth, they said, was the only home for life in the universe, the only place with air and water and sunshine so that life could begin and thrive. Now they are saying just the opposite: "There's life everywhere! It's all over the place!" What made them change their minds? What makes them so sure now that they are right?

Several events really. The first took place half a century ago and the most recent within the last dozen years or so.

Before Edwin Hubble (1889–1953) began his work with the great telescopes on Mt. Palomar in California in 1919, astronomers believed that our galaxy, the Milky Way, was the universe.

Then, in the mid-1920s, Hubble made a startling discovery. Not only had astronomers misread the Milky Way, he said, but

(*Top*) Coma cluster of galaxies. Edwin Hubble's discovery that faint smudges and blobs of light appearing on photographs of the heavens were entire galaxies was a startling breakthrough in astronomy. (*Kitt Peak National Observatory*) (*Bottom*) Andromeda Galaxy, the nearest galaxy in space to the Milky Way, resembles our galaxy in size and appearance.

the true universe was vastly—unimaginably—larger than anyone had ever dreamed!

Faint smudges that appeared in photographs of the heavens were not clouds of cosmic dust, as everyone thought, but entire galaxies—"island universes," he called them—great congregations of stars clustered together just the way stars clustered to form our own galaxy.

Within a galaxy, there could be millions, even billions, of solar systems like ours, nine planets orbiting a central star or sun. (A star "shines"—gives off heat and light and so is visible; but not even the most powerful telescopes have seen a planet outside our solar system. Planets are invisible "dark companions" of stars; they give off no light of their own.)

Using the Hale telescope with its massive 200-inch mirror —largest in the world—astronomers could count a *million galaxies* through the bowl of the Big Dipper alone! How many stars in an average galaxy? About 100 *billion!* In the universe? *One hundred thousand million billion!* (If you care to write out that figure, it's one followed by 20 zeroes!)

Numbers like this are so huge that they become meaningless. But if you will look at the photograph of the Andromeda Galaxy on page 19, you can get some idea of the number astronomers had begun talking about.

A faint patch of light in the night sky, Andromeda is about the size of the Milky Way, 100 to 200 billion stars. Some 2¼ million light-years away, it is the closest galaxy to our own in the cosmos—the universe.

Now imagine a hole the size of a pinprick anywhere in the cluster of stars in the photograph. If the photograph could be enlarged to Andromeda's true size in the heavens—a swatch of stars stretching trillions of miles—you would find that the pinprick had expanded to a hole so immense that it would have obliterated—wiped out—about one million stars as large as our star, the sun, and all the tens of thousands of planets in orbit around them. To cross from one edge of the "pinprick" to the other would take a spaceship traveling at the speed of light 700 years!

After telling his fellow astronomers about "island universes" in the cosmos, Hubble had still other startling announcements to make, for example, Earth's true position in the universe.

"Our sun," he said in effect, "is just an average star. In our immediate galactic neighborhood, there are 40,000 just like it. Sorry to have to tell you, but our solar system is no more in the middle of the universe than we are in the middle of the Milky Way. And the Milky Way is a pretty average-sized galaxy!"

Hubble pointed out that, in reality, our "average-sized galaxy" was a giant wagon wheel 100,000 light-years across and 25,000 light-years thick at the hub. Our solar system—our proud sun and its family of nine planets—occupied a spot in the suburbs so far out from the hub that light traveling at 186,000 miles per second takes 30,000 years to reach us from the center. (Distances in the universe are so immense that astronomers use "light-years" to measure them. The distance that light—fastest known thing in the universe—travels is about six trillion miles in one year. Thus, a star 50 light-years from the Earth is 50 x 6,000,000,000,000 miles away.)

Our position in the universe is so minute that, from Alpha Centauri—the closest star, a mere 4.3 light-years from Earth—our sun is only a bright point in the night sky, the sixth star in the constellation Cassiopeia. An astronomer standing on a planet orbiting Alpha Centauri and peering through a powerful telescope at our sun would not be able to see our solar system of nine planets orbiting this star or realize that, on the third planet out, intelligent creatures had built a highly technical civilization.

"We're in the galactic boondocks," said astronomer Carl Sagan from Cornell University, "where the action isn't!"

What did this new information about the universe tell astronomers? It told them that our proud Earth, far from being the kingdom of the universe, was hardly a dust mote afloat in the vast ocean of the cosmos.

"We must get used to the fact that we are peripheral," wrote astronomer Harlow Shapley (1885–1972), "that we move

(*Top*) Hub of the Milky Way. This photograph taken through a telescope shows only a small portion of the 100 to 200 billion stars in our galaxy. (*Kitt Peak National Observatory*)    (*Bottom*) The Whirlpool Galaxy, about 15 million light-years from Earth, has the appearance of a giant pinwheel. Young, hot stars in the "arms" create a fluorescent-like light on clouds of dust and chemicals in space between the stars. One "arm" reaches out to a smaller galaxy at the left. (*Kitt Peak National Observatory*)

along with our star, the Sun, in the outer part of a galaxy that is one among billions of star-rich galaxies."

It also suggested something else to astronomers. "Among all those billions of stars," they asked, "among all those solar systems, is it possible that life began only on Earth? Strange if it did because Nature never does anything just once. Nothing in nature is unique—the only one."

So Edwin Hubble a half century ago gave us a true picture of Earth's place in the universe and, in doing so, caused scientists to question that Earth was the only abode of life in the cosmos. Were scientists humbled by the knowledge that, instead of sitting on the throne of the universe, Earth occupied no more space than a sand grain on a thousand-mile beach?

Well, yes and no. About the time astronomers were reviewing these new findings, Albert Einstein attended a conference.

"To an astronomer," one scientist moaned to him, "man is nothing more than an insignificant dot in the universe."

Einstein frowned thoughtfully. "I have often felt that," he replied. "But then I realize that the insignificant dot who is man is also the astronomer."

## The Sphere in the Laboratory

Some 25 years after Hubble placed Earth in its proper position in the cosmic order, another event took place which astonished the scientific world.

In a laboratory at the University of Chicago, a young biologist-chemist, Dr. Stanley Miller, mixed ammonia, methane, water vapor, and hydrogen in a glass sphere and heated the brew to 180° C. for 18 hours. Two electrodes poked into the upper half of the sphere, and every so often 60,000 volts of "lightning" zapped between them.

What Dr. Miller was doing was reproducing the conditions on Earth when life first started some two to two-and-a-half billion years ago. The chemicals duplicated Earth's atmosphere at that time; the lightning flashes—actually a miniature storm in the sphere—provided heat.

At the end of the week, Dr. Miller stopped the experiment, opened a valve, and drained the sphere's contents. Placing drops of the brew under a microscope, he saw tiny amino acid molecules. These molecules—combinations of atoms—are the basic building blocks from which all life begins. Composed mostly of atoms of carbon, hydrogen, oxygen, and nitrogen, amino acids link together to form proteins. Proteins, in turn, promote tissue growth in plants and animals. Simple proteins have only four amino acids; others more complex may have 20.

Scientists recognized the importance of Dr. Miller's experiment. It showed how life could have begun on Earth from non-living matter. "No longer is the origin of life a deep mystery," said one scientist. "We have bridged, at least partly, the gap between life and the lifeless."

Applying Dr. Miller's work to Earth itself, scientists read the beginning of life as something like this:

About 4.6 billion years ago, Earth was formed and the stage was set for life to begin. Earth's atmosphere was a mixture of ammonia, methane, hydrogen, and water vapor. For two billion years these molecules drifted in the salty seas; each day the sun warmed them. Gradually the molecules came together and—aided by intense heat from lightning strokes—produced amino acids, the forerunner of proteins and life itself.

Hardly ten years after Dr. Miller's landmark experiment, scientists made another important discovery. "The chemicals that make up the building blocks of life are *not* confined to Earth," they said. "These same chemicals appear all over the universe!"

In 1963, Dr. Leonid Weliachew, of the California Institute of Technology, pointed a radio telescope at two galaxies each 10 million light-years from Earth and heard the first electronic whisperings of chemical molecules in space. When heated, a chemical atom or molecule in space becomes "excited" and gives off or "broadcasts" its own radio wave, which identifies it as accurately as a fingerprint identifies a human being. Radio telescopes—giant electronic "ears"—can hear radio waves coming to Earth from deep space.

THE SEARCH FOR LIFE ON OTHER WORLDS IN SPACE

"We once thought that the space between stars was empty," said one astronomer. "Now we find there are really great chemical factories in interstellar space that produce a thick alphabet soup. Already we have found H, C, O, and N—hydrogen, carbon, oxygen, and nitrogen."

In 1968, scientists at the University of California's Hat Creek Observatory pointed a radio telescope toward the center of the Milky Way and picked up signals given off by ammonia and water vapor.

Since then, scientists have identified about two dozen molecules in space including carbon monoxide, formaldehyde, hydrogen cyanide, and cyanogen.

Along with individual chemicals, astronomers discovered an entire cloud of methyl alcohol as big as our entire solar system floating in space—roughly 7,000 million miles wide. Molecules of methyl alcohol contain one carbon, one oxygen, and four hydrogen atoms. On Earth, molecules are plentiful. A child's thimble could hold a thousand billion. But in space, molecules are scarce. Maybe only one to ten would occupy the space inside the same thimble.

What did these discoveries mean to scientists?

"We know today," said one, "that all living things are made up of common chemical elements—about 65 percent oxygen, 18 percent carbon, 10 percent hydrogen, 3 percent nitrogen, and 2 percent calcium. The remaining 2 percent includes silicon, phosphorus, sodium, sulphur, iron, and a dozen other elements. All these chemicals are common in the crust of the Earth. Percentages vary, of course, in a trout and a chipmunk, or in a flea and the star quarterback on the football team. But all living things on Earth are composed of common atoms."

These discoveries meant simply this: If the molecules that created life on Earth are everywhere present in the universe, then something like what happened on Earth might have happened—perhaps millions of times—on other planets in the universe.

John Macvey wrote in his book *Alone in the Universe?*: "Does it . . . seem logical or reasonable to assume that this small planet tethered to an average star near the edge of an average galaxy should be the sole abode of life, intelligent or otherwise, in the universe?"

"It's easy to imagine laws of physics and chemistry that would not permit life," said Carl Sagan. "But we don't live in such a universe. We live in a universe remarkably hospitable to life."

In their exploration of the universe, astronomers came to realize another remarkable fact: The same physical laws that apply on Earth apply equally throughout the universe.

A chemistry teacher lecturing to students said: "Learn your biology and chemistry here and you will be able to pass examinations on Arcturus."

"In view of a common cosmic physics and chemistry," Harlow Shapley wrote, "should we not also expect to find animals and plants everywhere? It seems completely reasonable; and soon we shall say that it seems inevitable."

Life seekers are certain that, considering the billions of stars in the heavens and with favorable conditions, life elsewhere in the universe may be more the rule than the exception.

What are these favorable conditions? Certainly life can't evolve just anywhere. Some planets are simply not hospitable to life. What is it then about some planets—Earth is the best example we know—that welcomes and nurtures life? With billions of stars in the universe, how will we know which ones might have planets inhabited by intelligent beings for us to contact?

## The Meeting at Green Bank

In November 1961, eleven scientists met at the National Radio Astronomy Observatory at Green Bank, West Virginia. Some were astronomers; others were chemists, physicists, biologists, or mathematicians.

They met to discuss an important question: How many other worlds inhabited by intelligent beings might possibly exist in the Milky Way?

A great chemical factory and birthplace of stars, the Trifid Nebula in the constellation Sagittarius is a swirling ball of stars, dust, and glowing gas about 3,500 light-years distant. Gravity condenses the dust and gas; intense pressure ignites them. Our sun was born five billion years ago in just such a cloud. (*Kitt Peak National Observatory*)

"If a large number of other worlds exist," they said, "then we might find another civilization near Earth. But if only a small number exist—only a handful of civilizations among the millions of stars in the Milky Way—then we might be separated from other civilizations by tens of thousands of light-years. Trying to contact other intelligent beings in outer space might then be impractical."

To establish a figure for the possible number of civilizations in the Milky Way besides our own, they discussed the following factors:

• The rate at which new stars were born in the Milky Way during the period when our sun and its family of planets developed. "Probably one per year," they agreed.

• The fraction of these stars that formed *planets*. "It would be easy to calculate this figure," they said, "if all stars had planets, but not all do. There just isn't enough information available to answer this question. It may be that only one star in four or five has a family of planets."

• The number of planets per solar system with an environment suitable for life.

"The only basis for estimating this is our own solar system," the scientists said. "With quite an ordinary sun, we have two possible planets that might support life. One does, we know for sure—Earth. The other—Mars—we're not so sure about yet."

To survive, the scientists agreed, life requires the following conditions:

• A star must have a habitable zone, a wide belt of warmth neither too hot nor too cold for life. Earth is right in the center of our star's habitable zone. Venus and Mars also lie within this zone, Venus on the inside edge, Mars on the outer edge. At 5800° C., our star is midway in the temperature scale between very hot and very cool stars.

• A star must be long-lasting. Very large hot stars twice the size of our sun may live only two billion years, not long enough to give life a chance to develop. Small stars may have a very long life—100 billion years—but their habitable zone may be so narrow that the likelihood of a planet residing in it is slight.

• The heat output of a star must remain stable for billions of years to allow life to develop. About a third of Earth's 4.6 billion years was required for chemicals to organize themselves into cells and for life to begin. Our stable star has burned steadily at a constant temperature for at least five billion years and will stay the same, scientists estimate, for ten billion more.

• The temperature of a planet must stay within a range suitable for water to remain in liquid form. Generally, a constant temperature that caused water to boil or freeze would be unsuitable for life.

• A planet's size is important. It must be large enough to have a sufficient gravity to hold oxygen and other gases on its surface and to prevent these life-sustaining gases from drifting off into space. In contrast, meteors are too small to hold an atmosphere. Even our moon is too small. A planet's atmosphere also performs another role: it shields life against deadly ultraviolet rays from space.

• The orbit of a planet is critical. Earth moves in a nearly circular path around the sun; our temperature stays within a livable range. An oval orbit brings a planet too near its star and then takes it too far away. The temperature ranges from too hot to too cold for comfort and survival.

• Planets must have a fairly rapid rotation. If too slow, the temperature on the surface drops or rises to degrees dangerous for life.

Considering all elements necessary for a planet to have an environment suitable for life, the scientists finally decided: "Between one and five planets per solar system probably have an environment suitable for life to begin and thrive."

• But just because a few planets in a solar system developed environments suitable for life, does this necessarily mean that life will actually start and evolve on these planets? After much discussion, the scientists decided: On planets with suitable environments, life *had* to appear even if it took millions of years to get started. Where conditions for life were present, they said, life would inevitably begin.

• The number of life-bearing planets on which intelligence appeared. The scientists debated this question long and hard. Did life necessarily have to become intelligent? Couldn't fish remain fish or monkeys just stay monkeys? Finally, they decided that intelligence would appear sooner or later simply because the environment provided opportunities for intelligence to emerge. If life can thrive in the sea, they said, the life-force will adapt itself and fins will emerge. If life can exist in the sky, wings will emerge. What does the environment demand? If intelligence is demanded, in time and in one form or another intelligent life will emerge.

• The number of intelligent civilizations that have both the means and the desire to communicate with other worlds. A civilization might be highly advanced but be perfectly content within itself. If it didn't bother to develop the tools for interstellar communication (see next chapter), it would be impossible for us to communicate with it.

After much discussion, they decided that only 10 to 20 percent of civilizations with the equipment and desire to communicate would actually do so.

• The longevity of societies that have achieved nuclear technology. Do advanced societies eventually destroy themselves in nuclear warfare? If a society has the technology, that is, the nuclear weapons, to do so, some scientists thought that in time it would. Sooner or later a society would have to learn to control nuclear technology to survive. Those that did could survive indefinitely. Conclusion: "We either have to achieve a global society or perish."

(Eleven years after the Green Bank meeting, Dr. George Wald said to an audience at Boston University: "*Are* there advanced civilizations in outer space? Not that they have not existed, and I rather think they do exist, but how much farther do they get? Do they all produce hydrogen bombs and engage in cold wars and stockpile enough stuff to wipe out all life on the surface of these planets? Can we keep the show on the road much longer?" And Dr. Ronald N. Bracewell, Stanford University radio astronomer, wrote in his book *The Galactic Club*: "The explosive power of nuclear bombs is now equivalent to a ball of dynamite seven feet in diameter for each man, woman, and child on earth.")

How many societies "out there" had learned to live with nuclear energy? The scientists decided that 1,000 might represent the smallest number of societies in the Milky Way that had learned to live with nuclear energy and 100,000,000 might represent the greatest number.

What answer did the panel of scientists come up with? How many other worlds inhabited by intelligent beings might possibly exist in the Milky Way?

Actually, they came up with two answers—a minimum number and a maximum number. "In the Milky Way," they said, "our best estimates say there are somewhere between 40 civilizations and 50 million civilizations able and willing to communicate with us."

These findings, the panel of distinguished scientists felt, justified a search for intelligent beings on other planets in the galaxy.

### Life on Other Worlds: What's It Like?

One question facing scientists involved in the search for life on other worlds is: What will life out there be like? Like us? Different from us?

"I think it would mean something very like the life we know," said Dr. George Wald, Nobel Prize–winning biologist from Harvard University at the Life Beyond Earth conference at Boston University in November 1972. "Not the same creatures. . . . But life anywhere in the universe, I have been convinced for years, must be made of the same elements that principally constitute it here—carbon, hydrogen, nitrogen, and oxygen. These four elements constitute about 99% of living material on the Earth and I think are likely to come out that way wherever life exists."

We may have some similarity to other intelligent creatures in the universe. Other creatures will have brains, for example, and they must be able to move about and build things. So we can expect some kind of skull to protect their brains and limbs comparable to our hands and feet. They must have senses—vision, hearing, touch, and possibly other senses we know nothing about—to learn about the world in which they live. Their world will also have gravity; consequently, they need a bone structure or skeleton to support their body tissue and organs.

"If we should visit a planet essentially identical with ours in mass, temperature, age, and structure," wrote Harlow Shapley, "we should probably not find the biology queer beyond comprehension."

But we should expect differences, too. Like us, they will be the product of millions or billions of years of evolution, and they will reside on a planet whose environment is probably different from Earth's.

Our planet, for example, is composed of over two-thirds water. What about a planet that has far less water? Would creatures living there develop bulky bodies to store water and, like camels on Earth, carry around a life-sustaining supply?

On a planet whose gravity is less than Earth's, would creatures be taller than us, have lighter skeletons, weaker muscles? Gravity that pulled down less than ours would require less strength to resist it; consequently muscles and skeletons wouldn't have to be as strong and would grow more easily. On a planet with stronger gravity, would they have a sturdier bone structure, more powerful muscles, squatter bodies?

If the atmosphere on their planet is thin, will they have huge nostrils, large mouths, perhaps openings in their chests to pull in enough scarce air to enable their beings to function? It's possible because living creatures tend to adapt to the conditions of their environment.

To illustrate this law of nature, scientists performed a laboratory experiment with two salamanders, small lizards with four legs. One salamander was placed in a glass tank with little oxygen in the air; in time, the creature developed enlarged gills to take in more oxygen. The second salamander, in oxygen-rich air, reduced the size of its gills. Both creatures adjusted to the conditions of their world; intelligent beings make the same adjustment.

Some scientists feel that Earth has been extraordinarily blessed with light and color—the moon, for example, has only varying shades of gray and tan. Another planet may have dim light only. To see in dim light, that planet's residents would probably develop eyes the diameter of tea cups.

Then, too, our eyes are receptive to only a small portion of light waves in nature. We see "visible light"—from violet to red in the color spectrum—but are blind to infrared and ultraviolet waves. Our eyes function like a TV set that can receive signals on one or two channels without knowing about other channels available. But for earthlings this was no accident. Nature did not bother to equip us with vision unnecessary to our existence and survival. Beings on another planet, though, may be equipped with ultraviolet and infrared vision if seeing on these "channels" is necessary for survival there.

"The high probability in other creatures of senses unknown to us," said one astronomer, "seems reasonable. Many realities may lie beyond our comprehension simply because our senses are limited."

Probably the biggest surprise awaiting us, however, is meeting and getting to know intelligent beings whose civilization is much older—and hence more advanced—than ours.

Our galaxy, scientists point out, is about 10 billion years old. But Earth is only half that—roughly five billion years. So there are probably other worlds in the Milky Way that were formed millions or billions of years ahead of ours. Consequently, civilizations on these planets would be older and presumably more advanced than ours.

We have existed as a human species barely two million years. Our science is only 300 years old. We have been able to communicate by radio for about 50 years. Our ability to travel in space is but a few years old. If you can imagine what our science might be like in a hundred or, say, a thousand years, you will get a feeling for what civilizations only a few thousand years in advance of ours might be like.

There are also civilizations out there probably less advanced than ours. These planets might have creatures still living in caves, so to speak, to whom the printing press and electric light are still events in the distant future. But it's unlikely that our search will lead us to "backward" civilizations; they haven't developed the instruments to communicate over interstellar distances. These civilizations are most certainly in the cosmos, but we have no way of detecting them.

We might also be dealing with beings who are centuries old. Why? Because older civilizations would be skilled in the medical arts of prolonging life—replacing worn-out hearts, kidneys, and other organs, for example. Life spans of the average "person" might extend for hundreds of years.

"We are the product of 4.5 billion years of . . . slow, biological evolution," wrote Carl Sagan. "There is no reason to think that the evolutionary process has stopped. Man is a transitional animal. He is not the climax of creation."

How living creatures evolve—how we grew from simple beings into people who lived in caves and, from there, into more complex creatures who now are planning to visit other planets in space—is a process that scientists don't understand yet. But what they do understand is that we evolve in an orderly manner —there are no accidents or surprises in nature—and always from a crude form to a more advanced form.

One of the first scientists to investigate the process of how living things evolve from lower to higher forms was Charles Darwin (1809–1882). Darwin felt that a mysterious life force guided living things over generations to encourage their growth to more advanced forms. This life force, he claimed, had no description, no formula. But it guided the course of evolution of living things as surely as gentle and invisible gravity guided the stars and planets in their courses.

"There is a grandeur in this view of life . . ." he wrote in *On the Origin of Species*. "Whilst this planet has gone cycling on according to the fixed laws of gravity . . . endless [life] forms most beautiful and most wonderful have been and are being evolved."

Darwin was writing of the evolution of life on Earth, but we, with our new knowledge of the universe, might adopt his view and say that it applies equally well to life on other worlds in space.

# 4

# The Radio Telescope: Communicating with Other Worlds in Space

---

"It seems to us quite possible
that one-way radio messages are being beamed
at the earth at this moment
by radio transmitters on planets
around other stars."
—Frank Drake and Carl Sagan,
astronomers, Cornell University,
*Scientific American,* May 1975

---

"The instrument we will in all likelihood use to communicate with intelligent beings in other civilizations in space is the radio telescope," said an astronomer recently. "To an advanced civilization, radio may be as primitive as smoke signals are to us—there are some disadvantages in using it. But there are probably civilizations whose duty it is to look for other civilizations in the galaxy emerging into the communication stage—which means the radio telescope age. These civilizations are sure to use a radio telescope to communicate with 'the new kids on the block.'"

The mirror of the Hale telescope, the Western Hemisphere's largest optical telescope, located on Mount Palomar, California, collects starlight a million times fainter than that visible to the unaided eye. An observer (shown here sitting in the prime focus cage) photographs the image in the mirror.

The bottom photograph shows the massive Hale telescope pointing directly overhead through the open shutter in its protective dome.

Most people are familiar with optical telescopes, like the big 200-inch Hale telescope on Mt. Palomar in California. But the radio telescope is not such a familiar instrument.

Although they look different, radio telescopes and optical telescopes operate the same way: both collect and record electromagnetic waves coming to Earth from the universe. Optical telescopes collect light waves and radio telescopes collect radio waves.

To collect light waves, an optical telescope uses a large mirror. The mirror focuses the waves onto a photographic plate. Astronomers develop the plate and get a picture of what the telescope saw.

A radio telescope is a giant ear tuned on the universe. It collects radio waves—some as feeble as a millionth of a billionth of a watt—in a dish-shaped antenna. The antenna focuses the waves into a receiver. The receiver amplifies the signal— makes it louder—and records it on graph paper or displays it on a screen much like a TV screen. By examining the paper or screen, astronomers can "read" what the radio telescope heard.

Radio telescopes can do some things that optical telescopes cannot. They can be used day or night while optical telescopes are night instruments, to be used only when the stars come out. Nor do radio telescopes need to stand idle in cloudy weather that blinds optical telescopes. Radio waves pass through clouds and rain as if they didn't exist. They also penetrate gas and dust clouds floating in space that block or scatter light waves. In vain does the optical telescope try to peer through these interstellar clouds.

Best of all for life-seekers, the radio telescope can do one other thing that an optical telescope cannot: send messages. Today, the world's largest radio telescope at Arecibo, Puerto Rico, can beam a radio signal over a distance of 70,000 light-years. This means that it can send a message to a similar "ear" anywhere in the Milky Way. And even larger radio telescopes are being built or are on the drawing boards.

This radio telescope at the National Astronomy Observatory, Green Bank, West Virginia, collects feeble radio waves from space in a dish-shaped antenna almost two acres in size that focuses them on a receiver located at the top of the twin girders. Scientists in the control building (*bottom left*) study the waves that are recorded on graph paper or displayed on a TV-like viewing screen.

(*National Radio Astronomy Observatory*)

## Hissings from Space

As invaluable as it is to astronomers today, the radio tele-scope got its start quite by accident.

Early in the 1930s, Karl C. Jansky, a 25-year-old engineer with the Bell Telephone Laboratories in New Jersey, received an assignment from his boss: "Static is garbling our radio mes-sages over the Atlantic. Find out why!"

To study the problem, Jansky decided to record the static. In a field, he built a rickety antenna—copper wires strung on a wooden frame 100 feet long and 12 feet high—and attached four wheels from a Model-T Ford. An old gasoline engine pro-vided the power to turn the whole contraption on a track once every 20 minutes. As it rotated, the antenna scanned the entire sky for radio waves.

By August 1931, Jansky had discovered the cause of the static that was interfering with his company's radio messages—lightning in thunderstorms over the Atlantic. But during the months that he worked on the problem, he discovered some-thing else.

Below the crackling static he recorded, Jansky heard a strange sound. "Hissing," he called it. Another experimenter might have dismissed the sound, but Jansky was curious. Where did it come from? Somewhere in space certainly, because he recorded it at the same time he recorded the bothersome static.

In time, Jansky came to an astonishing answer. His awk-ward wood-and-wire antenna was actually collecting radio waves from outer space. And the waves came not only from the solar system, but from the core of the Milky Way 30,000 light-years away—a fact which he realized when he turned his crude antenna away from planets in our solar system and toward the center of the galaxy.

Jansky's curiosity had founded a new science—radio as-tronomy.

Within a few years, another experimenter carried Jansky's work a step further. In Wheaton, Illinois, Grote Reber, an amateur astronomer and radio "ham," read about Jansky's crude

(*Above*) A replica of the rickety wood-and-copper wire antenna built by Karl Jansky early in the 1930s that started the new science of radio astronomy. It is on display at the National Radio Astronomy Observatory, Green Bank, West Virginia. (*National Radio Astronomy Observatory*)    (*Below*) The radio telescope built by Grote Reber in 1936-37 was acquired by the National Radio Astronomy Observatory in 1958 both for its historical significance and for use in research. (*National Radio Astronomy Observatory*)

antenna. In 1936, he decided to build his own radio telescope. But Reber had a problem. The only space available to erect his antenna was the backyard of his home. So, instead of building an extended antenna like Jansky's, Reber solved his space problem by building a circular antenna 31 feet wide.

Reber's "dish" established the basic design for most of today's radio telescopes—a saucer-like antenna to collect radio waves and focus them on a receiver suspended just above the dish.

World War II interrupted further developments, but after the war astronomers immediately began working with this amazing new instrument for investigating the cosmos. Soon they were identifying sources of radio waves—stars, entire galaxies, faint clouds of interstellar gas—coming to Earth from outer space.

Because of the radio telescope's amazing ability to record radio waves, many astronomers were curious about using it for another purpose: to receive messages from other civilizations in the universe. "Messages may be passing all around us," they said, "and we don't know it!"

Among scientists, the idea of receiving radio messages from a civilization in space was not a new one. On at least four different occasions in the past scientists believed they had heard signals from extraterrestrial sources.

In 1899, Nikola Tesla, the brilliant and eccentric inventor of the electric motor, built a laboratory on a high plain near Colorado Springs, Colorado. He designed this special laboratory to study electrical disturbances in the skies above Earth. One day, his instruments registered signals that he described as interplanetary communication.

The signals took place "periodically," Tesla said, "and with such a clear suggestion of number and order that they were not traceable to any cause then known to me."

When asked if the signals were from the sun, the northern lights, or from Earth itself, Tesla replied: "I was as sure as I could be . . . that these variations were due to none of these causes."

What, then, did he make of the signals?

"Although I could not decipher their meaning," he said, "it was impossible for me to think of them as accidental. . . . [A] purpose was behind these signals. . . . They are the results of an attempt by some human beings, not of our world, to speak to us by signals. . . . I am absolutely certain they are not caused by anything terrestrial."

Twenty-two years later, in September 1921, Guglielmo Marconi, developer of wireless telegraphy, was working in a laboratory aboard his yacht *Electra* in the Mediterranean. One day he heard mysterious radio signals. The signals, he told H. C. H. MacBeth, manager of the London office of the Marconi Wireless Telegraph Company, were regular pulses, like code, and not electrical disturbances. "Marconi himself expressed the belief that the signals had originated . . . at some point in outer space," MacBeth later recalled.

In August 1924, Professor David Todd, an astronomer at Amherst College, used a new device to record radio signals. Called the "Jenkins Radio-Camera," the instrument was unusual in that it used a roll of photographic paper to record radio signals. Responding to the signals, a light beam flickered on and off and recorded them on an unwinding 16-inch roll of light-sensitive paper.

In late August, the U.S. Navy asked Todd to record signals that might come from the planet Mars as it approached within 35 million miles of Earth.

At the appointed time, Todd adjusted the antenna and waited. Then, to his surprise, the light began flickering in a regular pattern of dots and dashes. At intervals of about 30 minutes, the light flickered irregularly in clusters of signals. Listening posts in British Columbia, France, and England, using standard radio receivers, reported the regular signals but not the clusters of signals.

For 29 hours, Todd recorded the strange signals. When the photographic paper was developed, an astonishing pattern of regular signals emerged. Here is how *The New York Times* for August 28 reported the event:

"Development of a photographic film record of the radio signals . . . has deepened the mystery of the dots and dashes reported heard at the same time by widely separated operators of powerful stations.

"The film . . . discloses in black on white a fairly regular arrangement of dots and dashes along one side, but on the other side at almost evenly spaced intervals are curiously jumbled groups, each taking the form of a crudely drawn human face."

Scientists examined the paper and all asked the same question: Was this an attempt by extraterrestrial beings to contact Earth? They tried listening on the same radio wavelength again. But no more signals were heard—nor was there ever any explanation for the mysterious signals that had been recorded.

In October 1928, physicist Carl Størmer sent radio signals from Station PCJJ in Eindhoven in the southern Netherlands. Then Størmer and a fellow scientist named Hals heard mysterious echoes from the signals they had sent. The echoes varied between three and five seconds, but some came about eight seconds later.

At a distant receiving station, another physicist, Balthasar van der Pol, confirmed that he too had heard the echoes. "Last night . . ." he wired Størmer, "echoes here varying between 3 and 15 seconds, 50 percent of echoes heard after 8 seconds."

The "delayed echoes" were never adequately explained by scientists, and, six years later, echoes were heard once more, this time in Holland. That radio signals could seemingly be retransmitted back to Earth after delays of several seconds baffled scientists. The delays, they felt, could not be attributed to atmospheric quirks, magnetic storms, or other natural causes. "From where this echo comes I cannot say for the present," said one scientist. "I can only confirm that I really heard it."

Some 30 years later, one explanation for the "delayed echoes" was offered by Dr. Bracewell of Stanford University. Writing in *Nature*, a British science magazine, for May 28, 1960, Bracewell suggested that an extraterrestrial probe "sent here by our more advanced neighbors" might be the explanation for the strange echoes the scientists had heard.

Superior civilizations throughout the galaxy, he said, might already be linked in a galaxy-wide chain of communication. They keep watch on other solar systems by sending tiny spacecraft—probes—to orbit in the habitable zones of these solar systems. An unattended probe, computer equipped, armored against meteor strikes, and powered by the light of the star it was assigned to monitor, might circle within a solar system sentry-like for thousands of years. Then, when intelligent beings on a planet develop the know-how to send radio messages, the probe comes to life. It intercepts a sampling of messages and relays these signals to the home planet. The probe reports in effect, "Planet Earth is entering the radio technology stage of scientific development."

The echoes that bounce back to Earth might be the probe's way of announcing its presence to us—in effect, "You have been heard." But if this is true, why haven't we heard from the advanced civilization that sent the probe? Because the original radio message from Earth that the probe has relayed to its home planet might still be winging through space. Even at the speed of light, the message has traversed only 30 or so light-years. The home planet may lie 50 or 100 light-years away.

And so, in 1959, when the National Radio Astronomy Observatory at Green Bank, West Virginia, set up a brand-new radio telescope, astronomers who knew of past experiences with radio signals from space decided to make an experiment. Admiring the magnificent 85-foot dish tilted toward the heavens, they said something like, "Let's give it a try! Maybe there *is* someone out there sending signals, maybe even trying to get in touch with us!"

Dr. Frank Drake was in charge of the experiment, and he decided to call it Project Ozma. Based on the mythical land of Oz in *The Wizard of Oz*, the name, according to Dr. Drake, stood for "a place very far away, difficult to reach and populated by strange and exotic beings."

45

The steerable telescope at the National Radio Astronomy Observatory in West Virginia that Dr. Frank Drake used in 1960 for Project Ozma. Towering over its control building, the telescope stands 115 feet high and weighs 210 tons. (*National Radio Astronomy Observatory*)

## The Strange Signals

The National Radio Astronomy Observatory is located in a valley sheltered from man-made radio broadcasts by low mountains. For Project Ozma, Drake decided to concentrate on two nearby stars, Tau Ceti, 12 light-years away, and Epsilon Eridani, 11 light-years distant.

At 4:00 A.M. on April 8, 1960, final adjustments were made to the ultra-sensitive receiver, circuits were warmed, and the 85-foot dish swung slowly toward Tau Ceti just rising in the east above the mountains. Once on target and controlled by a clockwork mechanism, the antenna carefully followed the star across the sky.

In the control room near the dish, a loudspeaker broadcast Tau Ceti's hushed "breath." A recording pen, responding to the star's radio waves, traced peaks and valleys onto graph paper.

For hours the dish faithfully followed the star until, in midafternoon, Tau Ceti "set" behind the western mountains. No regular signals from the star—indicating a message—had been recorded.

Drake now ordered the antenna shifted to Epsilon Eridani, invisible in daylight. The dish released its hold on Tau Ceti, swung east, and locked on the star some 65 trillion miles out in space. Suddenly the loudspeaker in the control room crackled. The pen on the graph paper "went bang off scale," a startled observer said.

Quickly the volume was turned down, and all eyes stared at the graph paper. The pen was recording a series of regular pulses, about eight per second, uniformly spaced.

Everyone in the room shared the same astonishing thought. Was it possible that, on the second try, Project Ozma had found intelligent life in outer space and on a planet near a star that was a close neighbor?

Drake ordered the circuits checked. Everything was working perfectly. Just as he was about to make a final check—swinging the dish away from the signals; if they continued at the same strength, they came from a source on Earth; if they became weaker as the antenna swung past their source, they came from outer space—the signals stopped!

Five minutes of signals on the very first day! Yet Drake was reluctant to say they came from intelligent beings on another planet in space. He wanted more proof.

Each day for the next two weeks, Drake and his co-workers listened intently to Epsilon Eridani. They heard the star's regular "hash" of radio noise, but the signals did not come again. Drake was baffled. Then suddenly and with no warning, the loudspeaker crackled. The signals!

Quickly Drake steered the antenna away from Epsilon Eridani. Would the signals continue strong? Or would they weaken?

The signals continued to crackle from the speaker loud and clear. Investigation later revealed that a high-flying plane was broadcasting radio signals for a secret military experiment.

The truth of the signals was of course a great disappointment to Drake and his co-workers. Project Ozma ended—the new telescope was needed for other studies. But it was a gallant failure, humankind's first try at receiving a message from another world in space.

## The Big Ear

Nestled in a natural bowl of blue-green hills ten miles inland from the seacoast town of Arecibo, Puerto Rico, stands a marvel of modern cosmology, the world's largest radio telescope.

Probing farther into the universe than any of its smaller cousins, the Arecibo telescope has detected mountains beneath the 50-mile-thick cloud blanket covering Venus, mapped the moons of Jupiter, observed the rings of Saturn, identified life-forming molecules afloat in interstellar space, and beamed the first message into space to inform other civilizations in the universe that intelligent life exists on planet Earth.

"If the galactic community exists," said Arecibo's director, Dr. Frank Drake—the same Dr. Drake of Project Ozma—"we can now join it."

(*Above*) Cables from three towers of the Arecibo telescope, the world's largest radio telescope, located in Puerto Rico, suspend a triangular antenna platform 500 feet above the 1,000-foot-wide dish. (*Cornell University*)  (*Below*) To inspect the 38,778 aluminum panels that make up the Arecibo dish, workmen strap wide-soled footgear to their shoes. Holes permit rain to drain through the panels. (*Cornell University*)

Its transmitter—a single Klystron tube seven feet long and 18 inches in diameter that cost $125,000—is so powerful that it can zap a signal clear across the Milky Way. Its dish, a thousand feet wide, is sensitive enough to detect a baseball-size satellite circling the moon 240,000 miles away or to record the faint electronic hiss of a dying star on the edge of the universe.

When scientists selected a site on Mars for future space-craft landings (from photographs sent back to Earth from an orbiting Mariner spacecraft), the Arecibo telescope tested the site with its probing beam. Returning echoes indicated quick-sand. Scientists made up a batch of soil based on the echoes, placed a model of the future spacecraft on it, and then watched as it sank out of sight. Another landing site was then selected.

The dish of the Arecibo telescope is almost 20 acres in size and is made up of 38,778 aluminum panels, each 40 by 80 inches and ⅛ inch thick. Fine screws on each panel can adjust the dish to within three millimeters—about ⅒ inch—of a true sphere. This clean curve means clearer signals and gives as-tronomers the ability to pinpoint a radio source deep in space. The panels are holed to allow rain to drain through the dish and sunshine to warm plants growing below it. The plants serve a purpose: they prevent soil from washing away in the natural bowl in which the bowl hangs suspended.

In the Arecibo telescope, the huge dish acts as a reflector that gathers radio waves and focuses them on one of eight antennas hung from a platform 500 feet above the dish. The triangular antenna platform, 216 feet on a side, weighs 600 tons. It is supported by 3¼-inch-thick steel cables strung from three towers around the bowl. The largest antenna is 96 feet long and weighs five tons. Thirty-nine inch-thick steel cables, hung from concrete blocks around the dish's perimeter, keep the dish from swaying in gale-force winds and from changing shape as temperatures rise and fall.

The Arecibo telescope has one drawback, say astronomers who use it. But considering its overwhelming superiority over all other radio telescopes in the world, the fault is minor.

Suspended by steel cables 500 feet above the Arecibo dish, this 600-ton steel-girder platform holds eight antennas, the longest of which—pointing to the bottom of the picture—is 96 feet. (*Cornell University*)

Unlike dishes of other radio telescopes, the Arecibo dish is not movable—it is too heavy. Because the dish must stay in one position, the Arecibo telescope can record signals from only 39 percent of the heavens above it, considerably less than the near-complete coverage of smaller, movable, but less powerful telescopes.

### Let's Get Acquainted—But How?

If the radio telescope showed astronomers how to communicate with intelligent beings in other worlds in space, it also pointed out the practical difficulties of such an enterprise—not the least of which is using a radio telescope for listening purposes.

Since Project Ozma in 1960, astronomers in the United States have spent relatively little time listening for signals. In 1972, for example, two astronomers at the National Radio Astronomy Observatory began a project designed to listen to 600 nearby sun-like stars with a 300-foot dish. During the first two years, however, they logged a mere 400 hours listening time— about 16 days out of a possible 730.

Why so little time? One astronomer explained it this way:

"The time of radio telescopes is very valuable and we like to use them for projects which promise some return, some results. As fascinating as the search is for intelligent signals, it really doesn't offer that guarantee of results to justify the use of a valuable instrument. We have so many things yet to learn about space and what's happening out there. The radio telescope can help us learn what we want to know."

Scientists estimate that, even if a good-sized radio telescope were available full time, it might still take 10 to 30 years of 24-hour listening before a signal might be heard. If there are a million technical civilizations among the 100–200 billion stars in the Milky Way, astronomers say they must listen to about 200,000 stars for a fair chance of detecting a single message. By mid-1975, only a few more than 200 stars had been listened to.

Astronomers at Russia's Gorky Radiophysical Institute gen-

erally agree with this estimate. "Our most optimistic calculations say that hundreds of thousands to millions of stars will
have to be examined before an intelligent signal from one will
be heard," they have said.

But what if all civilizations in the universe are listening and
not one is sending? What do we do then?

If this is true, then the only way we will ever hear signals
from another civilization in space is through eavesdropping—
intergalactic snooping.

What this means, say scientists who support this idea, is
that any message we hear is likely to be accidental—not meant
for us. The message will be normal radio traffic between two
civilizations—a weather report, say, or the price of wheat, if
they grow wheat.

But eavesdropping is no easy task. It means pointing a radio
telescope at a promising star and then scanning a billion wave
lengths over which radio messages can be sent (although there
are some wave bands that may lend themselves more readily
than others to interstellar communication). Finding one "chan-
nel" being used by any civilization at any particular time is
obviously a long-term project.

And yet, a message from another civilization in space may
be speeding toward Earth at this very moment!

How could this happen? How could another civilization in
space know where to send a message?

Because, for the past 50 years, people from this planet have
been sending messages into space—commercial radio broadcasts
that began in the mid-1920s. These broadcasts have been ex-
panding wave-like from Earth at the speed of light since they
were originally broadcast and are now just about at the 50 light-
year marker. Most radio signals bounce back to Earth from
the ionosphere, the electrically charged outer layer of Earth's
atmosphere 30 to 250 miles up, but enough signals may leak
through to alert another civilization that intelligent life exists
on Earth.

A civilization in the 50 light-year range from Earth might

now be listening to the returns of the 1928 presidential election (Republican Herbert Hoover won over Democrat Alfred E. Smith), news of the stock market crash of 1929, or the results of the 1930 World Series (Philadelphia of the American League beat St. Louis of the National League four games to two to become World Champions).

If intelligent beings in this civilization in the 50 light-year range decided to introduce themselves to us by sending a radio message, it would take another 50 years for it to reach us—some time in the 2020s—and herein lies the greatest difficulty in communicating with other civilizations in the universe: distance.

Cosmic distances across which radio signals must speed, even at 186,000 miles per second, are so vast that the human mind can't embrace them.

Consider our solar system only—our "family" of nine planets orbiting an average-size star. Yet our star is so huge that, if it were cut in half and one side hollowed out, our planet and our moon 240,000 miles away in space could still fit inside the half-sphere!

If the sun were reduced to the size of a grapefruit and placed at the tip of the Washington Monument and other planets were reduced accordingly, Earth would be a sand grain 40 feet away. Pluto, the outermost planet, would be another sand grain about two city blocks away. But the nearest star, another grapefruit, would be 2,000 miles away in Phoenix, Arizona. In the real universe, a particle of light from this nearest star, Alpha Centauri, takes four years and four months to arrive at Earth. At the time that particle left Alpha Centauri, you finished the eighth grade, and by the time it arrived on Earth, you had graduated from high school. And that's the distance between Earth and the star *nearest* to us!

When you look at the famous North Star, the particles of light—photons—striking your eye started out 680 years earlier, about 200 years before Columbus discovered America. If you happen to be looking at the star at 10:30 or 11:00 P.M., the light entering your eye was passing Pluto's orbit, 3,577,000,000 miles away, some five and one-half hours earlier, about the time you were eating your evening meal.

Yet, in the immense universe, the North Star is hardly in the next backyard. To get to the center of our galaxy, we would have to zip along on a light beam for 30,000 years; to cross it, for 100,000 years!

If, among the 100–200 billion stars in our galaxy, a million civilizations exist—a reasonable guess, astronomers say—and if they are evenly distributed throughout the Milky Way, the distance between the nearest civilization and Earth would be 300 light-years. This means that, if we asked a question, it would take 300 years for our query to get there and another 300 years, a total of 600, for an answer to come back. It's even possible that we could receive a message from a distant civilization that no longer exists—the message zinging through space while, behind it, that civilization destroys itself in an all-out nuclear war.

So distance between worlds in space and time needed to transmit messages between them is the major difficulty in space communication. But most important events in history take years —even centuries—to develop. Our history books, for example, make the settling of America look like a sudden event. In reality, however, it took over a century. After Columbus discovered America, 113 years passed before the Pilgrims came to these shores in 1605.

There is always the chance, too, that the time-distance factor will be overcome by new high-speed communication devices. Even now there may be a solution to the problem waiting to be discovered.

Recent experiments have shown that tiny particles may exist whose *slowest* speed is that of light. These particles—called tachyons (the Greek *tachys—fast* or *swift*)—actually loaf along at 186,000 miles per second. Scientists suspect that tachyons in full flight may be a *billion* times faster than photons. Right now, tachyons exist on paper only as mathematical equations, the usual first step before scientists prove their existence in fact.

For space communication, the value of tachyons is obvious.

A message formerly requiring 300 years to be "delivered" at the speed of light may, at tachyon speed, require only hours or minutes. Hard to believe, it's true. But then we seem to say this about most things in this new science of exobiology.

## The New Ears

On a 7,000-foot-high plateau surrounded by low mountains 20 miles west of the old mining town of Magdalena, New Mexico, the National Science Foundation is erecting not one but 27 radio telescopes.

Called Very Large Array, the project will consist of 82-foot dishes riding railroad flat cars along three tracks in the form of a Y. The southeast and southwest arms of the Y will extend 13 miles each; the northern arm, 11.8 miles. The tracks will cross private ranches, one county line, and U.S. Highway 60. Railway gates will halt cars and trucks when the traveling telescopes—hauled at 5 m.p.h. by 70-ton diesel-electric transporters running on second parallel tracks—creep across the highway.

"There's a clear view for ten miles in either direction, so there shouldn't be any problem with traffic," said an engineer working on the project. "But I sure bet we see some surprised motorists!"

Scheduled for completion in 1981, the VLA will be the equivalent of a radio "ear" almost 26 miles in diameter. Nine telescopes to a leg will allow a new observing technique called "aperture-synthesis."

This new technique will allow faint radio waves striking several antennas at the same time to be combined into one common image. With the receiving dishes miles apart, all focused on the same target, the sharpness of the image becomes, as one astronomer said, "exquisite!" Pictures may even be as clear as those taken by large optical telescopes.

With an ear as sensitive as this, scientists will be able to distinguish radio waves from a pinpoint of light among millions of other stars. The VLA will also be able to map gas clouds between stars—"giant chemical factories," scientists call them—

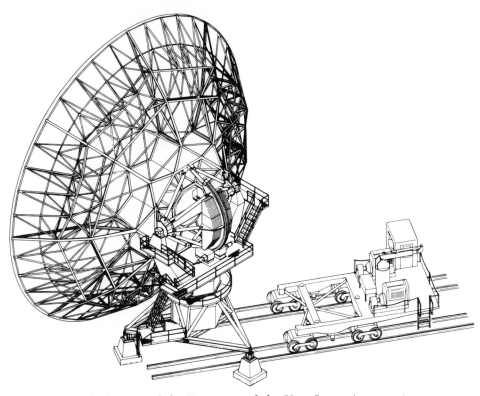

(*Top*) An artist's drawing of the Y-juncture of the Very Large Array project. Radio telescopes, delivered to their positions by diesel-electric transporters, stand on spur tracks set at right angles to the three arms of the Y. U.S. Highway 60 crosses one arm at the bottom left. (*National Science Foundation*)
(*Bottom*) A drawing of one 82-foot radio telescope in the Very Large Array project and its 70-ton diesel-electric transporter. (*National Science Foundation*)

with such detail that processes taking place inside clouds will become visible.

"I believe this instrument is going to revolutionize radio astronomy," said David S. Heeschen, Director of the National Radio Astronomy Observatory.

And according to the National Academy of Sciences: "Such a giant step in capability will certainly produce major discoveries and surprises that cannot be predicted."

The VLA concept is remarkable indeed, but an even larger network of radio telescopes may be on the way. The National Aeronautics and Space Administration has proposed a project that would require between 1,000 and 2,500 radio telescopes! Their primary purpose: "to communicate with intelligent life beyond Earth." The plan is called Project Cyclops.

In size and complexity, Project Cyclops dwarfs any research instrument yet devised. From the air, the array of telescopes would cover a circular area of 25 square miles. The 330-foot telescopes—each wider than a football field is long—would be connected to each other and to a computer in a control building located in the center of the array. The computer would direct the hundreds of antennas to scan band widths most likely to be used for interstellar communication and search through them for signals indicating some mark of intelligence. Finally, the computer would analyze all data and print a report that would allow scientists to see what intelligent signals might have been received.

The combined telescopes would be capable of detecting signals from intelligent beings that may already be coming to Earth amidst all the radio "hash" from the universe, eavesdrop on daily communications between civilizations in space, and pick up such relatively weak signals as local radio or TV "programs" from a civilization within several hundred light-years of Earth.

With an effective range of about 1,000 light-years, the telescopes could also be used for making fine radar studies of bodies in the Milky Way and for tracking our space probes to distances far beyond the radio range of present telescopes. The

(*Above*) An artist's drawing of the 1,000 to 2,500 radio telescopes that would combine in Project Cyclops to listen for, and record signals from, intelligent civilizations within 1,000 light-years of Earth. A control building is located in the center of the array. (*National Aeronautics and Space Administration*)
(*Below*) An artist's drawing showing a ground-eye view of the 330-foot radio telescopes proposed for Project Cyclops. The centrally located control building appears at lower right. (*National Aeronautics and Space Administration*)

estimated cost of building the telescopes is $10 to $20 billion. Construction time: 20 to 30 years.

"The search for extraterrestrial life," the NASA report on Project Cyclops stated, "is a legitimate scientific undertaking and should be included as part of a comprehensive and balanced space program."

## Numbers into Pictures

Saturday, November 16, 1974, was an important date in the history of humankind's quest to communicate with beings on other planets in space. In the early afternoon on this date, the first radio message from Earth deliberately intended to communicate with intelligent beings elsewhere in the universe left Earth in a three-minute burst of 1,679 pulses. The message was aimed at a cluster of 300,000 stars in the Milky Way known as Messier 13. This star cluster with its invisible planets is 25,000 light-years from Earth.

"I would say there is about a one in two chance of there being a civilization in Messier 13," said one of the scientists who sent the message.

The occasion for the message was the dedication of the Arecibo radio telescope after a three-year work project had stripped the big dish of its original wire mesh antenna, installed 11 years earlier, and replaced it with 38,778 aluminum panels.

"This opens a new era in radio astronomy," said a scientist who spoke to 250 people gathered for the ceremony. "The Arecibo dish will probe farther into the universe than any instrument ever built by man."

A siren wailed a warning, and people in the hot Puerto Rican sun watched as the powerful Klystron tube transmitter pointed directly at the center of Messier 13.

Then the message began. At the rate of ten characters per second, the message took just 169 seconds to transmit. One person said it sounded like "an eerie whine, rising and falling, like strange music played on a giant electronic organ with only two notes."

```
0 0 0 0 0 0 1 0 1 0 1 0 1 0 0 0 0 0 0 0 0 0 0 0 0 1 0 1 0 0 0 0 0 1 0 1 0
0 0 0 0 0 0 1 0 0 1 0 0 0 1 0 0 0 1 0 0 0 1 0 0 1 0 1 1 0 0 1 0 1 0 1 0 1
0 1 0 1 0 1 0 1 0 0 1 0 0 1 0 0 1 0 0 0 0 0 0 0 0 0 0 0 0 0 0 0 0 0 0 0 0
0 0 0 0 0 0 0 0 0 0 0 0 0 0 1 1 0 0 0 0 0 0 0 0 0 0 0 0 0 0 0 0 0 0 0 0 0
1 1 0 1 0 0 0 0 0 0 0 0 0 0 0 0 0 0 0 0 0 1 1 0 1 0 0 0 0 0 0 0 0 0 0 0 0
0 0 0 0 0 0 0 1 0 1 0 1 0 0 0 0 0 0 0 0 0 0 0 0 0 0 0 0 0 0 1 1 1 1 1 0
0 0 0 0 0 0 0 0 0 0 0 0 0 0 0 0 0 0 0 0 0 0 0 0 0 0 0 0 1 1 0 0 0 0
1 1 1 0 0 0 1 1 0 0 0 0 1 1 0 0 1 0 0 0 0 0 0 0 0 0 0 0 0 1 1 0 0 1 0
0 0 0 1 1 0 1 0 0 0 1 1 0 0 0 1 1 0 0 0 0 1 1 0 1 0 1 1 1 1 0 1 1 1 1 1
0 1 1 1 1 1 0 1 1 1 1 1 0 0 0 0 0 0 0 0 0 0 0 0 0 0 0 0 0 0 0 0 0 0 0 0
0 1 0 0 0 0 0 0 0 0 0 0 0 0 0 0 0 1 0 0 0 0 0 0 0 0 0 0 0 0 0 0 0 0 0 0
0 0 0 0 0 0 0 0 0 1 0 0 0 0 0 0 0 0 0 0 0 0 0 0 0 0 0 0 0 0 1 1 1 1 1 0 0
0 0 0 0 0 0 0 0 0 0 1 1 1 1 0 0 0 0 0 0 0 0 0 0 0 0 0 0 0 0 0 0 0 0 0 0
0 0 1 1 0 0 0 0 1 1 0 0 0 0 1 1 1 0 0 0 1 1 0 0 0 1 0 0 0 0 0 0 0 1 0 0 0
0 0 0 0 0 1 0 0 0 0 1 1 0 1 0 0 0 0 1 1 0 0 0 1 1 1 0 0 1 1 0 1 0 1 1 1
1 1 0 1 1 1 1 1 0 1 1 1 1 1 0 1 1 1 1 1 1 0 0 0 0 0 0 0 0 0 0 0 0 0 0 0
0 0 0 0 0 0 0 0 1 0 0 0 0 0 1 1 0 0 0 0 0 0 0 0 1 0 0 0 0 0 0 0 0 0
0 0 1 1 0 0 0 0 0 0 0 0 0 0 0 1 0 0 0 0 0 1 1 0 0 0 0 0 0 0 0 0 0
1 1 1 1 1 0 0 0 0 0 1 1 0 0 0 0 0 0 1 1 1 1 0 0 0 0 0 0 0 0 0 0 0 1 1 0
0 0 0 0 0 0 0 0 0 0 0 1 0 0 0 0 0 0 0 1 0 0 0 0 0 0 0 1 0 0 0 0 0 1
0 0 0 0 0 0 1 1 0 0 0 0 0 0 1 0 0 0 0 0 0 0 1 1 0 0 0 1 1 0 0 0 0 0 0
1 0 0 0 0 0 0 0 1 1 0 0 0 1 0 0 0 0 1 1 0 0 0 0 0 0 0 0 0 0 0 0 0 0 0
0 1 1 0 0 1 1 0 0 0 0 0 0 0 0 0 0 0 1 1 0 0 0 1 0 0 0 0 1 1 0 0 0 0 0
0 0 0 0 1 1 0 0 0 0 1 1 0 0 0 0 0 0 1 0 0 0 0 0 0 0 1 0 0 0 0 0 0 1 0 0 0
0 0 0 0 0 1 0 0 0 0 0 1 0 0 0 0 0 0 0 1 1 0 0 0 0 0 0 0 0 1 0 0 0 1 0 0 0
0 0 0 0 1 1 0 0 0 0 0 0 0 1 0 0 0 1 0 0 0 0 0 0 0 0 1 0 0 0 0 0 0 0
1 0 0 0 0 0 1 0 0 0 0 0 0 0 1 0 0 0 0 0 0 1 0 0 0 0 0 0 1 0 0 0 0 0 0
0 0 0 0 0 0 1 1 0 0 0 0 0 0 0 0 1 1 0 0 0 0 0 0 0 1 1 0 0 0 0 0 0 0
0 1 0 0 0 1 1 1 0 1 0 1 1 0 0 0 0 0 0 0 0 0 0 1 0 0 0 0 0 0 0 1 0 0 0 0
0 0 0 0 0 0 0 0 0 1 0 0 0 0 0 0 1 1 1 1 0 0 0 0 0 0 0 0 0 0 0 0 0 1 0 0 0
0 1 0 1 1 1 0 1 0 0 1 0 1 1 0 1 1 0 0 0 0 1 0 0 1 1 1 0 0 1 0 0 1 1 1
1 1 1 1 0 1 1 1 0 0 0 0 1 1 1 0 0 0 0 1 1 0 1 1 1 0 0 0 0 0 0 0 0 0 1 0
1 0 0 0 0 0 1 1 1 0 1 1 0 0 1 0 0 0 0 0 0 1 0 1 0 0 0 0 0 1 1 1 1 1 1 0 0
1 0 0 0 0 0 0 1 0 1 0 0 0 0 0 1 1 0 0 0 0 0 0 1 0 0 0 0 0 1 1 0 1 1 0 0 0
0 0 0 0 0 0 0 0 0 0 0 0 0 0 0 0 0 0 0 0 0 0 0 0 0 0 0 0 0 0 0 1 1 1 0 0
0 0 0 1 0 0 0 0 0 0 0 0 0 0 0 0 0 1 1 1 0 1 0 1 0 0 0 1 0 1 0 1 0 1 0 1
0 1 0 0 1 1 1 0 0 0 0 0 0 0 0 1 0 1 0 1 0 1 0 0 0 0 0 0 0 0 0 0 0 0 0
0 0 1 0 1 0 0 0 0 0 0 0 0 0 0 0 0 1 1 1 1 0 0 0 0 0 0 0 0 0 0 0 0 0
0 0 0 1 1 1 1 1 1 1 1 1 0 0 0 0 0 0 0 0 0 0 0 1 1 1 0 0 0 0 0 0 0 1 1 1
0 0 0 0 0 0 0 0 1 1 0 0 0 0 0 0 0 0 0 0 1 1 0 0 0 0 0 0 1 1 0 1 0 0
0 0 0 0 0 0 1 0 1 1 0 0 0 0 0 1 1 0 0 1 1 0 0 0 0 0 0 1 1 0 0 1 1 0 0
0 0 1 0 0 0 1 0 1 0 0 0 0 0 1 0 1 0 0 0 1 0 0 0 1 0 0 0 1 0 0 1 0 0 0 1
0 0 1 0 0 0 1 0 0 0 0 0 0 0 0 0 1 0 0 0 1 0 1 0 0 0 1 0 0 0 1 0 0 0 0 0 0 0 0
0 1 0 0 0 0 1 0 0 0 0 1 0 0 0 0 0 0 0 0 0 0 1 0 0 0 0 0 0 0 0 1 0 0
0 0 0 0 0 0 0 0 0 0 0 1 0 0 1 0 1 0 0 0 0 0 0 0 0 0 0 0 1 1 1 0 0 1 1
1 1 1 0 1 0 0 1 1 1 1 0 0 0
```

(*Illustration above and on next page*)   The Arecibo message is decoded by arranging the 1,679 pulses into 73 groups of 23 characters each and placing one group under the other. The result is a visual message that can be interpreted by making each "0" represent a white square and each "1" a black square. (*Cornell University*)

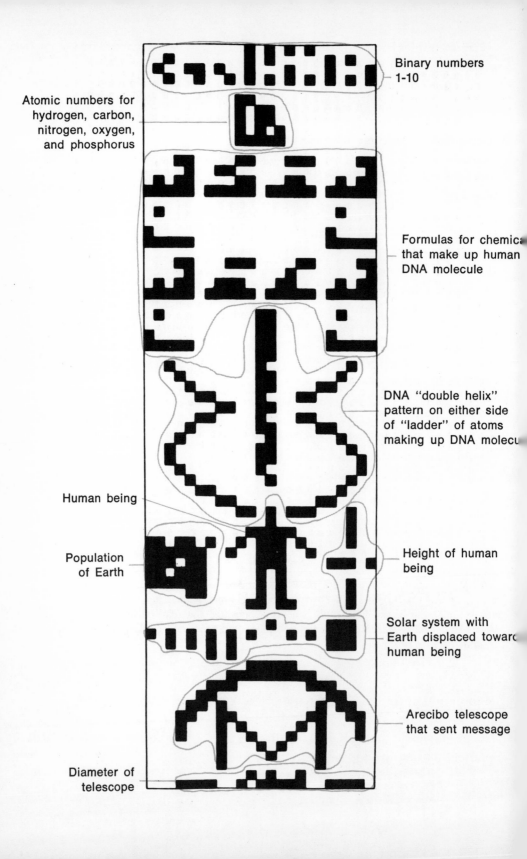

Binary numbers 1-10

Atomic numbers for hydrogen, carbon, nitrogen, oxygen, and phosphorus

Formulas for chemic: that make up human DNA molecule

DNA "double helix" pattern on either side of "ladder" of atoms making up DNA molecu

Human being

Population of Earth

Height of human being

Solar system with Earth displaced towar human being

Arecibo telescope that sent message

Diameter of telescope

The two notes represented binary numbers—numbers written with only two symbols: high and low notes or pulses.

The 1,679 pulses made up a figure that can be divided by two prime numbers only: 23 and 73. Scientists at the National Astronomy and Ionosphere Center at Cornell University who operate the telescope hoped that another civilization, recording the high and low pulses in their receiver, would recognize that they formed a grid 23 pulses wide and 73 long. On a grid, one frequency note would represent an "O" or white square; the second frequency note would represent a "1" or black square. Filling in the appropriate squares on the grid would reveal the message. (See page 62.)

"It's really an anti-puzzle," said NAIC's director, Dr. Frank Drake. "It's a code designed to be easily broken."

The message begins simply, with binary numbers from one to ten. Once other creatures recognize this key, they will be able to decode the rest of the message.

The next group of black squares describes chemicals that abound in living creatures on Earth—actually the atomic numbers for hydrogen, carbon, nitrogen, oxygen, and phosphorus. Since these numbers should be the same on the receiving planet as they are on Earth—representing the same elements (although they will have different names)—scientists there should have no difficulty recognizing them.

Then comes a diagram of something more complex—a picture of the human DNA molecule. This master molecule controls the form, operating mechanisms, and behavior of all human beings on Earth. This shape, too, should be recognizable to scientists on other planets. Between the "double helix" pattern is a "ladder" of four billion atoms that make up the DNA molecule in humans.

The DNA molecule leads to a rough sketch of a human being. To the figure's right is a number representing Earth's population: four billion. To its left is a number indicating the figure's height: about five feet, ten inches.

Below the human figure appears our solar system—nine planets with some suggestion of relative sizes. The large sun is at the right. Earth is slightly elevated to indicate something special about it, the home planet of the figure above.

Finally, near the bottom of the grid, there appears a picture of the instrument that sent the message. Numbers at the lower edge indicate the instrument's size.

Will the message ever be received and decoded? Chances are good because, by the time the message arrives at Messier 13, the beam will have spread to take in the entire cluster of 300,000 stars. Although the message was sent only once at the dedication ceremony, it will be repeated whenever the telescope is not being used for other work.

Unfortunately, though, we will never know if anyone reads the message because it won't arrive until the year 26,974. To get an answer will require another 26,000 to 27,000 years.

Why did astronomers select a cluster of stars so far away from Earth at which to beam the message? Wasn't a closer target available, one from which we might expect an answer within, say, a hundred years or so?

"There was no closer target available, at the time of the ceremony, which contained as many stars within the antenna beam," said Dr. Drake. "The message was both serious and ceremonial and the most propitious target was chosen."

The message left Earth at 1:30 P.M. Thirty-five minutes later it had passed Jupiter's orbit; 71 minutes later, Saturn's orbit. In the early evening, as the 250 guests at the dedication ceremony boarded buses for the trip back to town—five hours and 20 minutes after the message was sent—it had passed Pluto's orbit and was heading out of the solar system.

The people paused before boarding the buses. Above the dark hills surrounding the giant telescopes, Messier 13 was just becoming visible in the night sky.

# 5

# "Have You Looked Over the Edge of the Universe?"

---

"As scientists and dreamers,
we are curious about our position
in the plan of the universe."
—Harlow Shapley, *Of Stars and Men*

---

In 1783 on a visit to Paris, Benjamin Franklin saw the first public launching of a hydrogen-filled balloon.

"What in heaven's name is it good for?" someone in the crowd asked.

The 77-year-old statesman had witnessed many sights during his eventful life. He wasn't quite as ready as the skeptical onlooker to dismiss this new invention.

"Of what use is a newborn babe?" he replied.

Michael Faraday (1791–1867), an English scientist, was an early experimenter with electricity. One day a pompous Member of Parliament interrupted his work. Pointing a walking stick at the mess of magnets, wire, and copper discs on Faraday's workbench, he said, "Could this—these *things* have any possible value?"

Faraday considered the plump politician. How could he explain the value of something that didn't exist? Someday electricity would be a useful tool, a new form of energy, a work-saver. But this man who lived only in the present, who had no vision, couldn't possibly understand this. Faraday could offer a promise only; the politician wanted hard facts. Since politicians were always looking for new ways to tax the people for more money to run the government, Faraday smiled and said sweetly, "Sir, someday you may be able to tax it."

These two incidents from history make an important point for our story: Of what value is our search for extraterrestrial life? If intelligent beings exist on other planets in space, what possible contribution can they make to our lives on planet Earth? Think of the enormous amount of time, thought, and money being consumed to locate life out there!

"Read the daily paper!" say skeptics. "You'll find plenty of problems for bright young scientists to handle—pollution, over-population, the energy shortage, hunger in half the world's countries, dwindling natural resources. There's plenty to do right here on good old Earth! Now, tell me, what good is it going to do us to spend time—years maybe—listening for a few beeps from space?"

How do scientists and other life-seekers answer the skeptic's question?

There are many answers, and the first one is simple: Scientists don't know yet how we'll benefit.

"When you're looking for new information, for new knowledge," they say, "you can't require first that you'll know in advance what the results will be. If you make a condition like this—to know what you're going to learn before you begin—you put a block on the experiment before you even start out!"

Norman Cousins, a famous editor, commented in his magazine, *Saturday Review*, about this very situation:

"Research is at its best, not when everyone knows exactly what the research will yield, but when investigators are free to test their assumptions and to pursue their hunches. Goals in science are of primary value when they inspire pursuit."

## Questions to Ask

If scientists had an opportunity to do so, what questions would they ask intelligent beings who live elsewhere in the universe?

"Life in another world would presumably be at a far more advanced state of evolution—technological, biological, medical —than ours," wrote science writer Walter Sullivan in his book *We Are Not Alone.* "Knowledge of such a civilization, its discoveries, its techniques, might enable us to leapfrog thousands or even millions of years ahead along the path before us."

But scientists would try to avoid asking questions the answers to which will probably be discovered here on Earth—a cure for cancer, for example. By the time the answer comes to us, in a century, say, we will have discovered the cure ourselves. "When we read the answers," they say, "we don't want to be embarrassed by our questions."

Some scientists, like Dr. Melvin Calvin, Nobel Prize winner and Director of the Laboratory of Chemical Biodynamics, University of California, Berkeley, would ask questions requiring a technical answer.

"I suppose the principal question to which I would like an answer," Dr. Calvin said, "is what is the nature of their life's chemistry. By this I mean what are the elements upon which their structures are built and the kinds of molecules into which they have been incorporated as well as how they work—including various life functions, metabolism, nervous system, etc."

Other scientists would ask questions about the vast and unknown universe in which we live.

• Where do comets come from? From outer space, or are they "born" within a solar system?

• Why are the nine planets in our solar system—from Mercury to Pluto—spaced out from our star, the sun, as they are? How did they find their precise positions in space?

• How did the universe begin—and how old is it? Scientists on Earth have pushed the age of the universe steadily backward. The latest figure is 18 billion years calculated by Dr. Allan Sandage, Hale Observatories, California. Correct? Or is the universe still older?

- Have you mapped the universe? What is its shape and size?

- Is there an edge to the universe? Our telescopes show the most distant object to be 10 to 12 billion light-years away and beyond that—nothing. Have we seen the edge of the universe? What lies beyond?

- We have partial—and incomplete—answers to *what* the universe is and *how* it works. But to the question "*Why* is the universe?" we have no answer at all. Do you? (A physicist at a large eastern university put the question this way: "I would like to know the answer to the greatest mystery of all—why there is something rather than nothing!")

- Have you discovered life on other planets besides Earth? "Knowing we are not alone would change our entire outlook on life," said one scientist. "We would realize we are part of a cosmic community."

- Is it possible to travel through the universe at the speed of light? Faster than light?

- Why do some stars blow themselves to pieces in stupendous explosions?

- What is a quasar? Small objects spotted throughout the universe, quasars give off tremendous energy. "A quasar gives off in one second more energy than we on Earth consume in a billion years," said George M. Low, deputy administrator of NASA. "Surely we would like to tap that secret."

Some scientists say a quasar is "the brilliant central core of some much larger object, perhaps the core of a galaxy about to be born." How true is this?

- "Maybe we could find out what gravity is and how to control it," said a scientist.

Gravity is the feeblest, and perhaps most awesome, of nature's powers. The gravitational energy of Earth amounts to only a millionth of a horsepower—a toy magnet is stronger. Yet this weak force controls the universe. According to Isaac Asimov, professor of biochemistry at Boston University, "It governs the way in which planets circle suns, in which stars circle each other, in which whole clusters of stars cling together by the millions and even trillions, in which galaxies themselves move among each other . . ."

Relentless, inexhaustible, it will cling to a bubble with an invisible leash or penetrate a thousand-mile-thick cube of lead. It can't be stopped or slowed down. We can control other forms of energy—electricity, nuclear energy, heat, light—with the flick of a switch. But gravity has defied both control and explanation.

"Gravity is one of nature's most baffling forces," scientists say. "If someday we can overcome gravity by developing an anti-gravity device, we might be able to travel at incredibly fast speeds. If intelligent beings from advanced civilizations can travel between solar systems, maybe they use anti-gravity propulsion."

• Have you ever found a way out of a "black hole"? Has anyone ever survived after being trapped in one?

Discovered only a few years ago, a black hole is the most mysterious object in the universe. John G. Taylor, Professor of Mathematics, King's College, London, described it this way in his book *Black Holes: The End of the Universe?*: ". . . man is now in the position of facing the ultimate unknowable which can never be penetrated as long as he remains in his present physical form. That ultimate unknowable is the black hole. However hard he may struggle he will never be able to get out of this most fearsome object of the heavens once inside it. Nor can he ever find out what is happening in its interior if he stays outside, fearing to make the one-way trip."

A black hole results from a star, three or four times the size of our sun, whose nuclear energy over billions of years finally exhausts itself and it goes "out"—stops shining. Its energy expended, with nothing to counterbalance the pull of its own gravity, the star collapses into itself. Requiring less than a second, the collapse is so fast that we couldn't see the star in the process of "winking out" and vanishing.

Consumed by its own gravity, the star becomes an invisible "hole" in the sky, a black hole because not even light can escape its clutch. A spaceship flying too near would be sucked into its maw, like a matchstick into a whirlpool, never to escape again. Nor could space travelers aboard the doomed craft send out an SOS and hope for rescue. Powerful gravity would hold even radio signals inside.

But fearsome as black holes are, some scientists feel they may play an unexpected role in the universe. A black hole, they say, may be a "pipeline" to another part of the universe thousands of light-years away—enter one end and, microseconds later, you get blown out the other end. Black holes may be the highways by which spacecraft from advanced civilizations travel throughout the universe.

It may also be possible, they say, to enter a black hole in this universe and emerge from a "white hole" in another universe. Black holes may be the way we'll eventually discover what lies beyond the "edge" of our universe.

Sound strange, weird even? Remember that black holes are not the wild imaginings of science-fiction writers but the sober speculations of serious scientists who hold responsible positions in great universities. Long study of the universe makes them agree with a remark once made by the late British scientist J. B. S. Haldane.

"The universe," Haldane said, "is not only queerer than we suppose, but queerer than we can suppose."

## Surprises Await

Is there any chance that a more advanced civilization would attack Earth and make us slaves? After all, advanced scientific knowledge could mean advanced weapons for warfare.

"We do not need to fear attack by other civilizations," said Dr. Frank Drake. "The vast distances separating the stars create a very effective quarantine, making competition between civili-

zations unproductive. In this matter, space is not like the earth
—we need not worry that the advanced will subjugate the less
developed. . . . Overall, human life should be greatly en-
riched by being exposed to the variety of intelligent beings,
life styles, art forms, and technologies which we will learn of."

"The knowledge of science and technology to be ex-
changed . . . would be endlessly intriguing," stated Kendrick
Frazier, editor of *Science News,* "but for my money I would
like . . . to be an anthropologist. . . . Think of the questions
to be asked and the things to be learned! What is their language
like? How do they govern themselves? . . . Do they have fam-
ilies? Cities? Nations? What are their ideals, their philosophies?
What do they do for fun? What is their art . . . like? Do they
have wars? What are their concepts of work? These are just a
few of the questions, but what's interesting is to realize that
we will undoubtedly be surprised: the most revolutionary answers will come to questions we never anticipated asking. And
that is the whole point. There will be entirely other ways of
thinking."

With maybe a half-smile, Dr. Lewis Thomas, a biologist,
suggested in his book *The Lives of a Cell* that "the safest thing
to do at the outset . . . is to send music." He felt that the
"language" of music would best explain to others what people
on Earth were really like. The music of Johann Sebastian Bach
would be best suited for this purpose, Dr. Thomas stated. Many
musicians consider Bach our greatest composer. "We would be
bragging, of course, but it is surely excusable for us to put the
best possible face on at the beginning of such an acquaintance."

Could other beings help us with what Norman Cousins
called "the most serious problem on earth"?

"If other galaxies have civilizations that are unmarked by
brutality and violence," he wrote, "it would be useful to know
how this came about. The inhumanity of humans to one another
continues to be the most serious problem on earth."

When we see how different other intelligent beings are
from us, will we be drawn together? Will our disputes with

each other, because of race, religion, and nationality, end as we see our common similarities as earthlings? Some thoughtful people feel the brotherhood of all people and nations will at last come about when we confront other life forms that are entirely different.

The greatest benefit, though, may be in our recognition that we are kin to all living things, both on Earth and in the universe.

"We've all grown up with the notion that people are totally separate," wrote Dr. Lewis Thomas in *The Lives of a Cell*, "—a very special form of life with no connection with the rest of life beyond ownership of it. That we're a 'chosen species.' That the whole place was meant for us to use as we please. . . . I deplore such a proprietary role. We don't own the place, we're an indivisible part of it!"

Biologists now believe we are on the threshold of discovering how all life is interconnected. All life forms, they say—plant, animal, and human, the grasshopper and the geranium, the eagle and the oak, a Norwegian, a Chinese, a gypsy, as well as intelligent creatures in other worlds in space—are made of the same star-stuff, a pinch of carbon, a whiff of oxygen and hydrogen, a drop of water. The only difference is the amount and proportion of these elements.

"The deeper we look into nature," wrote the great humanitarian Albert Schweitzer, "the more profoundly we know that . . . we are united with all life."

And Harlow Shapley: "To be a participant [in life] is in itself a glory. With our confrères on distant planets; with our fellow animals and plants of land, air, and sea; with the rocks and waters of all planetary crusts, and the photons and atoms that make up the stars—with all these we are associated in an existence and an evolution that inspires respect and deep reverence. We cannot escape humility. And as groping philosophers and scientists, we are thankful for the mysteries that still lie beyond our grasp."

Is there a conflict with religion in the discovery of intelligent beings on other planets? Is our God the God of other beings as well?

In the mid-nineteenth century, Father Angelo Secchi, a priest and an astronomer, asked himself if God had populated only one tiny speck in the universe—Earth—with spiritual beings.

"It would seem absurd to find nothing but uninhabited deserts in these limitless regions," he wrote. "No! These worlds are bound to be populated by creatures capable of recognizing, honoring and loving their Creator."

Some who heard William Ralph Inge, Dean of St. Paul's Cathedral in London, lecture in the 1930s on extraterrestrial beings felt he might have been a trifle less blunt.

Is there "soul-life in all parts of the universe?" Inge asked his audience. "There may be, and no doubt are, an immense number of souls in the universe, and some of them may be nearer to the divine mind than we are!"

Most scientists and religious people agree that "a one-planet God" has little appeal and that the God of humanity is equally the God of gravitation, other galaxies, and other beings. That God should favor Earth and human beings above other beings and places in the universe smacks of a conceit that without doubt isn't justified.

"The Universe that lies about us," wrote Walter Sullivan, "visible only in the privacy, the intimacy of night, is incomprehensibly vast. Yet the conclusion that life exists across this vastness seems inescapable. We cannot yet be sure whether or not it lies within reach, but in any case we are a part of it all; we are not alone."

# 6

# The Cosmic Greeting Card

"We are on the threshold
of a preliminary reconnaissance of the cosmos.
For the first time in his history,
Man is capable of sending his instruments
and himself from his home planet
to explore the universe
around him."
—Carl Sagan, *The Cosmic Connection*

On March 3, 1972, Pioneer 10—a 570-pound spacecraft with a dish-shaped antenna—was launched from Cape Kennedy. The destination of the tiny craft: Jupiter, fifth planet from the sun. Its mission: to photograph the orange-and-blue striped sphere and radio the photographs, in electronic "bits" or signals, back to Earth, where a computer would assemble them into recognizable photographs.

After orbiting Earth, the tiny spacecraft put on a burst of speed and left Earth's gravity at 31,122 m.p.h.—8.65 miles per second.

Eighty-three days later, the $50 million craft passed the orbit of Mars. By mid-August, it entered the 175-million-mile-wide Asteroid Belt, a thick wheel of dust and rocks. The largest asteroid is about the size of Minnesota. Others are barn size and range down to flinty dust specks. Collision with even a pea-

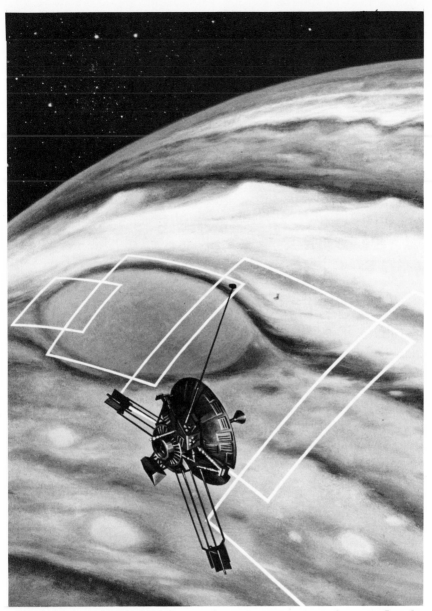

An artist's drawing of the 570-pound Pioneer 10 spacecraft as it flew by Jupiter. The overlapping squares show areas scanned by the craft's camera and by that of Pioneer 11 in December 1974. Stars shine in the area at the upper left. (*National Aeronautics and Space Administration*)

sized asteroid—holing its shell and damaging delicate instruments—would have destroyed the speeding craft.

By Thanksgiving Day 1973, Pioneer 10 was still seven million miles from Jupiter and beginning to accelerate in the pull of the big planet's gravity. Far behind the racing spacecraft, Earth was a distant silver dot on the edge of the sun's glare.

Within one million miles of the planet, Pioneer crossed the orbits of Jupiter's 12 moons, two of which are larger than our moon. Its radio was now sending 1,024 bits each second. After a 400-million-mile, 46-minute passage back to Earth, the faint signals reached a waiting 210-foot antenna at Goldstone, California.

At 6:25 P.M., on December 3, only one minute off schedule 21 months after launching, Pioneer passed within 81,000 miles of Jupiter. Every $1/1,000$ of a second, its camera recorded the planet in 64 shades of red and blue. The shadings were stored in the spacecraft's tiny computer, then sent back to Earth in bursts of 1,000 bits per second. The signals were reproduced in shades of red and blue to produce two-color photographs.

As it flew past Jupiter—at 86,900 miles in diameter the largest planet in our solar system—Pioneer 10 revealed information about the planet not known before. Its great mass—more than twice the material of all other planets in our solar system—had a gravity pull two and a half times more than Earth's. "That's strong enough to flatten Earth's mountain ranges!" said one surprised scientist. An outer gas envelope—hydrogen, helium, ammonia, methane, and water—contained the same elements thought to have triggered life on Earth.

Pioneer had approached the big planet at 20,000 m.p.h. Now Jupiter's powerful gravity grasped the frail craft and whipped it off into space at 82,800 m.p.h., the first man-made object to head out of the solar system.

By 1979, Pioneer will reach the orbit of Uranus—1.7 billion miles from Earth—where the thread of radio communication will finally cease. Eight years later, in 1987, the silent craft will cross the orbit of Pluto, the farthest outpost of our solar system,

3.6 billion miles from Earth, the edge of deep space.

Now a space derelict free of the sun's gravity, ghosting along at 23 miles per second, Pioneer will head into the Milky Way in the general direction of Taurus, a seven-star constellation near Orion and Aries.

But for the craft to arrive in the general neighborhood of these stars will take some 80,000 centuries. Said one scientist: "Pioneer 10 may just cruise between the stars until the end of time."

As Pioneer sails along on the longest space mission in history, NASA scientists hope the tiny craft will perform one more service—notify intelligent beings elsewhere in space that intelligent life exists on Earth. Bolted to an antenna-support strut is a six- by nine-inch gold-coated aluminum plate on which a message is permanently etched. "It's like tossing a bottle with a message into the ocean," scientists said. "Maybe someone someday will find it."

The message of the plaque (see page 78) should be decoded easily by any intelligent creatures who intercept the spacecraft.

• Two symbols at upper left show two states of the hydrogen atom. To scientists elsewhere, they will indicate a unit of time (radio frequency) and distance (wavelength). This symbol should be recognized immediately because hydrogen is the most widespread element in the universe.

• A starlike diagram shows Earth's position in space in relation to 14 pulsars—stars that send off radio pulses at regular intervals.

• The long horizontal line extending to the right behind the two figures shows the direction to the center of the Milky Way.

• To give an idea of human dimensions, the two figures stand in front of a diagram of Pioneer 10 with its dish-shaped antenna. The figures are not shown holding hands; others might see this as one creature joined together at the fingers. (Because they had never seen a horse, the Aztecs and Incas saw Spanish soldiers on horses as one animal with two heads.) The

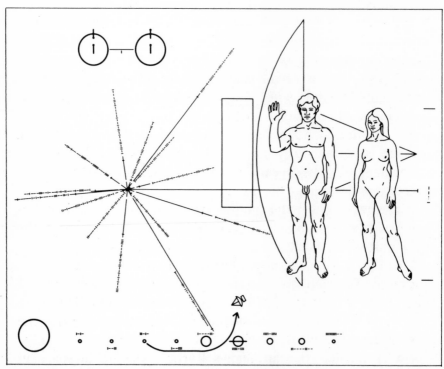

This message to extraterrestrial beings was etched on a 6-by-9-inch gold-coated aluminum plate bolted to one of Pioneer 10's antenna support struts. (*National Aeronautics and Space Administration*)

man's right hand is raised in a sign of goodwill. Only one figure is shown with an arm raised so other intelligent beings will not think some of us have one arm permanently bent.

• Across the bottom of the plaque is a diagram of our solar system. The sun is at left. The diagram shows that Pioneer 10 was launched from the third planet out from the sun and then was passed out of the solar system by the fifth planet's gravity.

(A year after Pioneer 10 left Earth, Pioneer 11 followed carrying an identical plaque. In December 1974, Pioneer 11 came within 26,600 miles of Jupiter, orbited it for 52 hours taking pictures, then was slingshotted toward Saturn. It will reach this planet in 1979 before heading out of the solar system. At the time the mission was planned, Pioneer 11's path around Saturn was not anticipated. Consequently, intelligent beings who someday might intercept Pioneer 11 somewhere in the galaxy may be baffled by the spacecraft's location and its line of flight in relation to the information clearly inscribed on the plaque that says it passed out of Jupiter's orbit. Another mystery of the universe, but this one for other intelligent beings to ponder!)

"Any creatures who intercept Pioneer 10 in space will be smart enough to figure out the plaque," scientists say. "It tells them from what planet in the universe the craft came from, when it was launched, and who launched it. Actually, the message specifies one star in about 250 billion and one year—1970—in 10 billion. The figures will probably be the most difficult symbols to understand because the creatures who intercept Pioneer 10 probably won't look like us."

The plaque will undoubtedly be the longest-lived work of the human race. It may survive for billions of years. When the Rocky Mountains have ground down to molehills, when human beings have long since colonized other planets, the tiny plaque will continue to exist, perhaps still gliding swiftly through space on its silent carrier, a cosmic greeting card from intelligent beings on one planet who wanted to share knowledge of themselves with other intelligent beings in the universe.

# Bibliography

---

## Books

Allen, Tom. *The Quest: A Report on Extraterrestrial Life.* Philadelphia: Chilton Books, 1965.

Angrist, Stanley W. *Other Worlds, Other Beings.* New York: Thomas Y. Crowell Company, 1973.

Berendzen, Richard, ed. *Life Beyond Earth & the Mind of Man.* Washington, D.C.: National Aeronautics and Space Administration (NASA SP–328), 1973.

Bergier, Jacques. *Extraterrestrial Intervention.* Chicago: Henry Regnery Company, 1974.

Bracewell, Ronald N. *The Galactic Club.* San Francisco: W. H. Freeman and Company, 1975.

Condon, Edward U. *Scientific Study of Unidentified Flying Objects.* New York: Bantam Books, 1969.

Dole, Stephen H., and Asimov, Isaac. *Planets for Man.* New York: Random House, 1964.

Fuller, John G. *Aliens in the Skies.* New York: G. P. Putnam's Sons, 1969.

Jastrow, Robert. *Red Giants and White Dwarfs.* rev. ed. New York: Harper & Row, 1971.

Keyhoe, Donald E. *Flying Saucers from Outer Space.* New York: Holt, Rinehart and Winston, 1953.

Levitt, I. M. *Beyond the Known Universe.* New York: Viking Press, 1974.

Macvey, John W. *Alone in the Universe?* New York: Macmillan Company, 1963.

Macvey, John W. *Whispers from Space.* New York: Macmillan Company, 1973.

Nicolson, Iain. *Simple Astronomy*. New York: Charles Scribner's Sons, 1973.

Sagan, Carl. *The Cosmic Connection: An Extraterrestrial Perspective.* New York: Doubleday & Company, 1973.

Shapley, Harlow. *Of Stars and Men*. rev. ed. Boston: Beacon Press, 1964.

Sullivan, Walter. *We Are Not Alone: The Search for Intelligent Life on Other Worlds*. New York: McGraw-Hill Book Company, 1965.

Taylor, John G. *Black Holes: The End of the Universe?* New York: Random House, 1973.

von Ditfurth, Hoimar. *Children of the Universe*. New York: Atheneum Publishers, 1974.

# Periodicals

*Reader's Guide to Periodical Literature* supplied titles of magazine articles published over the past ten years for this book—a list too long to be included here. But readers interested in the subject of extraterrestrial life can consult the *Reader's Guide*—available in most libraries—under the following subjects:

Astronomers through Astrophysics
Cosmology
Flying Saucers
Galaxies
Interstellar Communications
Life on Other Planets
Milky Way
Radio Astronomy
Radio Telescopes
Space Astronomy
Space Flight
Space, Outer
Telescopes
Telescopes on Space Vehicles
Universe

For non-scientists, the *Reader's Guide* is the single best source to use in order to keep up to date on this fascinating subject.

# Index

# INDEX

# INDEX

National Academy of Sciences, 3, 58
National Aeronautics and Space Administration, 58, 60, 68, 77
National Astronomy and Ionosphere Center, 63
National Radio Astronomy Observatory, 26, 45, 47, 52, 58
and life-in-space conference, 26-31
radio telescope, 45-48
National Science Foundation, 56
*Nature*, 44
*New York Herald*, 12
*New York Times*, 43-44

Oannes, 11
Oberth, Hermann, 6, 14
*On the Origin of Species*, 35

Pioneer 10, 74-79
Pioneer 11, 79
Project Cyclops, 58-60
Project Ozma, 45-48

Quasar, 68

Radio telescopes, 24, 25, 36
Arecibo, 38, 48-52, 60-64
development of, 40-42
eavesdropping by, 53
Green Bank (National Radio Astronomy Observatory), 45-48
how they work, 38
Project Cyclops, 58-60
Project Ozma, 45-48
Very Large Array, 56-58
Reber, Grote, 40-42

Sagan, Carl, 21, 26, 34, 36, 74
Sandage, Allan, 68
Schweitzer, Albert, 72
*Scientific American*, 36
Secchi, Angelo, 73
Shapley, Harlow, 21-23, 26, 32, 65, 72
Størmer, Carl, 44
Sullivan, Walter, 67, 73
Sumer, 10-11

Tachyons, 55-56
Tau Ceti, 47
Taylor, John G., 18, 69
Telescopes
optical, 38
radio. *See* Radio telescopes
Tesla, Nikola, 42-43
Thomas, Lewis, 71, 72
Todd, David, 43-44

Unidentified Flying Objects
American Institute of Aeronautics and Astronautics, statement by, 7-8
Arnold, Ken, sighting by, 6, 10
astronauts' reports of, 9
Condon, Edward U., report by, 7, 9-10
Cooper, Gordon, statement by, 13
explanations for, 13-16
foo fighters, 12
hallucinations, 7, 14
hoaxes, 7
Hynek, J. Allen, statement by, 14
Macvey, John W., statement by, 14
McDonald, James, statement by, 14-15
Mead, Margaret, statements by, 13, 15
misidentifications, 7, 13-14
Oberth, Hermann, statement by, 14
sightings, 8-13
U.S. Air Force study of, 6-10
Ziegel, Felix, statement by, 13
Universe, 20, 21, 23, 68, 70

Van der Pol, Balthasar, 44
Very Large Array radio telescope, 56-58
Von Littrow, Joseph, 2

Wald, George, 30-31, 31-32
*We Are Not Alone*, 67
Weliachew, Leonid, 24
Winthrop, John, 12

Ziegel, Felix, 13

85